The Whole World Goes to Hunter

The Whole World Goes to Hunter

Creating a Culture of Excellence and Activism, 1870–1964

LAURA S. SCHOR

excelsior editions

Cover credit: Cover image of Hunter College "Park Ave. N.E. Cor. 68th St." Ewing Galloway, NY. Courtesy of the New York Public Library.

Published by State University of New York Press, Albany

Printed in the United States of America

EU GPSR Authorised Representative:
Logos Europe, 9 rue Nicolas Poussin, 17000, La Rochelle, France
contact@logoseurope.eu

Excelsior Editions is an imprint of State University of New York Press

For information, contact State University of New York Press, Albany, NY
www.sunypress.edu

Library of Congress Cataloging-in-Publication Data

Name: Schor, Laura S., author.
Title: The whole world goes to Hunter : Creating a culture of excellence and activism, 1870–1964 / Laura S. Schor.
Description: Albany : State University of New York Press, [2026]. | Series: Excelsior Editions | Includes bibliographical references and index.
Identifiers: ISBN 9798855805949 (pbk. : alk. paper) | ISBN 9798855807172 (epub) | ISBN 9798855805956 (PDF)
Further information is available at the Library of Congress.

To Hunter students—past, present, and future.

Mihi cura futuri

The care of the future is mine.

Contents

Illustrations

Acknowledgments

This book begins with a thank you to Flora Tristan, the French Peruvian activist, who advocated for a universal workers' union of men and women in her book *The Workers Union*, which was published in 1843. I came across Tristan in a footnote while studying for my PhD orals fifty-five years ago. I questioned why I hadn't read anything about her during my studies and was eager to learn more about this remarkable woman and her ideas. Reading about Tristan was my entry into the nascent field of women's history. My dissertation about the women silk workers of Lyon was inspired by Tristan's description of the conditions of these workers. For several decades I taught and did research about women and girls. During those years I wrote five books about nineteenth-century French women and girls and later two books about women and girls in twentieth-century Jerusalem.

This book, my first foray into American history research and writing, began in the seminar room of the Hunter College Archives. In September 2022 I taught an honors class, Writing Women's Biography, to a group of eleven Hunter College students. We met weekly in the seminar room, surrounded by boxes of archival material. Students were required to write a brief biography of a Hunter alumna using letters, essays, stories, and photographs they discovered in those boxes. Before the class began, I spent a few weeks familiarizing myself with the organization of the Hunter Archives and began to compose a list of alumnae who had donated their papers to the archives. In addition to the papers about individual graduates, there were decades of yearbooks, literary magazines, and newsletters to read. My students, struggling to meet a variety of personal and political challenges, were quickly engaged in the stories of former students who had faced the challenges of World War I, the Depression, World War II, McCarthyism, sexism, and racism. Their enthusiasm for learning more about the history of Hunter College and its students inspired me to write this book.

When the semester ended, I was committed to writing a book about the history of Hunter College when it was a women's college. Many years earlier, I had read Mary McCarthy's novel, *The Group*, about eight young women who graduated from Vassar in 1933. My book would be a history of "the other group"—including Catholic, Jewish, and Black students—who couldn't afford tuition at Vassar or other selective women's colleges, and who wouldn't have been welcomed into those elite institutions. I wanted to profile the heterogeneous Hunter students who had helped to create a culture of excellence and activism that remains the foundation of the college more than 150 years after its first students graduated.

Several colleagues and friends were helpful as I navigated this new challenge. Three deserve special mention: Jane Bowers, who directed the Women's Studies program at Hunter in the late 1990s; Ann Kirschner, who was interim president of Hunter College during the time I did the research for this book; and Deborah Gardner, who is historian and curator at Roosevelt House. All three were familiar with the college and its students. They were devoted readers of the manuscript. Each offered thoughtful advice. Their enthusiasm for telling the story of the Hunter students of old soon matched my own. I have also benefited from the advice of Lewis Goldfrank, my partner, who read and reread each chapter as I continued to revise. His keen interest in the story of each alumna inspired me to continue my pursuit of elusive details about their lives and to find a way to tell their history.

Research about the history of Hunter College could not have been accomplished without the resources of the Hunter College Archives, established by President John Meng in a letter to the faculty of September 25, 1961. Meng announced the appointment of Professor Dorothy G. Fowler of the History Department as college historian, explaining: "What we need and what we do not now have is a useable collection of papers of more than passing significance to illustrate policy decisions and other determinations and events of general importance for future reference—in short, to document the institutional history of the college, so far as we can do it with what we possess and what we continue to accumulate."

President Meng began the process of creating the Hunter College Archives, which continues today with the small staff of Philip Swan, head,

Hunter College Archives and Special Collections, and archivists Susan Kline and Wendy Jimenez. Their efforts to bring out box after box of material for me to review and their searches for missing copies of publications were professional and collegial. I am deeply grateful to them.

Introduction

In December 1942 three Hunter students—Dorothy Freedman, Sonya Boekman, and Grace Fillyo—contributed an essay to the student literary magazine, the *Echo*, titled "The Whole World Goes to Hunter," celebrating the diversity of students attending their college. From its beginning in 1870, the admissions policy of Hunter College, then called the Female Normal College, had invited all girls, specifically Catholic, Jewish, and Black students, to apply. Though the early students were primarily daughters of middle-class white Protestants, in the ensuing decades a potpourri of students of different social classes, ethnic, racial, and religious backgrounds took advantage of the welcoming policy and free tuition to attend Hunter College. The three students profiled in the article included a Polish British Jewish immigrant who arrived in New York after a long separation from her family, a Chinese immigrant who relocated with a large family from California, and a Dutch immigrant whose accent was a source of mirth for all her friends. All three participated in college life and were deeply attached to their classmates. They were also keenly aware of the worlds they had left behind and provided a personal perspective on the international crises of their time.

The students enrolled at Hunter were originally called "girls" by everyone. President Thomas Hunter, faculty, students, and alumnae all used the term to describe Hunter students. In the early decades, before there were public high schools, the students were quite young, some even younger than the minimum age requirement of fourteen. In later decades, students started college after graduating from high school, thus they were likely to be in their late teens or early twenties when they graduated. Nevertheless, students continued to refer to themselves as "girls" through

World War II. I have adopted their nomenclature until chapter 5, which deals with the 1950s, at which point there was a slow transition to identifying Hunter students as women.

Similarly, there was general acceptance of the term "colored" to identify students of African American heritage in the early decades of the college. Later, students of color and others adopted the use of Negro and later still of African American or Black. I have followed the historical usage as it changed at Hunter. Finally, I have used the term "chairman" to refer to both men and women department leaders, as it was used at Hunter during the years under review.

This book describes the culture of Hunter College, a public women's college, as it evolved from its founding in 1870 until 1964, when it became coeducational. In its early decades, the college had an important place in the life of the city. At first called the Female Normal College, indicating its role as a teacher training institution, it was renamed Hunter College, in honor of its founder, Thomas Hunter, in 1914. The college was frequently mentioned in newspaper accounts celebrating its milestones in education, sports, and culture. Its graduation ceremonies, debates, and athletic meets were covered in *The New York Herald*, the *New York Post*, *The New York Times*, and other local newspapers. Its annual SING and Varsity programs were reviewed. The activities of college alumnae, who established the Lenox Hill Settlement House, the Northrup Memorial Summer Camp, the Patriotic Service Committee, the War Bond Committee, and scholarship and welfare funds, were discussed in the news of the day. In 1943, a civic committee that included several alumnae purchased the double townhouse on East Sixty-Fifth Street that had been home to Sara Delano Roosevelt (Franklin Roosevelt's mother) and to Eleanor and Franklin Roosevelt. The Sara Delano Roosevelt Memorial House (later, Roosevelt House) was used to foster interreligious and interracial cooperation by providing club rooms for Hunter's social clubs. The opening ceremonies featuring Eleanor Roosevelt were widely reviewed in the press. Today, the unique contributions of Hunter College to the education of over sixty thousand women from 1870 to 1964, and the noteworthy contributions of those graduates have faded from memory. The achievements and struggles of the college have largely been ignored in the secondary literature about American women's colleges. This lamentable lacuna in the history of American higher education is redressed here in the story of the evolution of the college and the contributions of some of its extraordinary students.

I was only somewhat aware of the unique culture of the college when I arrived at Hunter in August 1989 to serve as provost and senior vice president for academic affairs, a position I held for nine years. A quarter century after the college became coeducational, I found an unusually strong group of women in leadership positions among the senior administrators, department heads, faculty, and students. In the quarter century after I left the administration at Hunter, I studied the storied leaders, faculty, students, and alumnae. I was able to immerse myself in the culture of the college as reported in student newspapers, literary journals, yearbooks, and alumnae newsletters preserved in the Hunter archives. Memoirs by and biographies of distinguished alumnae added to my trove of information. In a small number of cases, I was able to interview alumnae whose memories of their college years remained vivid. The reference section at the end of this book gives direction to those seeking additional information.

My first interview with an alumna took place shortly after I arrived at Hunter. I was advised by a seasoned colleague to meet Ruth Goldstein Weintraub, class of 1925. No longer physically robust, Ruth remained intellectually engaged with many faculty following her retirement in 1972. She lived close enough to Hunter for friends to drop in with news and to seek her advice. Born Ruth Goldstein in 1905, she was the youngest of three children who grew up on the Lower East Side. Her father was a tailor. Her older sister, Gertrude, went to work to help support the family. Her older brother, Harold, graduated from City College. Ruth felt privileged to attend Hunter College.

She was an excellent student and a participant in a variety of student activities. Elected president of her freshman class and vice-president of her sophomore class, she served on the junior prom committee, was the circulation manager and business manager for the yearbook, and was a member of the Social Science Club, the Honor Board, and the Curriculum Committee. She was a member of the Pi Sigma Alpha political science honorary society as well as a member of Phi Beta Kappa.

Ruth began her lengthy career at Hunter in 1926 as a tutor in the History and Social Science Department. In 1930 she was one of the first women to graduate from NYU Law School. She also earned a PhD in political science from Columbia in 1939. At Hunter, she was promoted to professor and went on to serve as chairman of the Political Science Department, dean of graduate studies in the Arts and Sciences, and as the founding dean of the Division of Social Sciences.

My meeting with Dean Weintraub took place in her home, across Central Park from the Hunter campus. We drank tea as she reminisced about the challenges she had overcome in her decades of various leadership roles at Hunter. She encouraged me to be bold, to reject resistance to change. In the coming weeks and months whenever I encountered unwillingness to try new solutions to old problems, I remembered her advice. Dean Weintraub modeled the culture of excellence and activism she had learned as a Hunter student. She became an accomplished administrator by remaining true to these values. She was also remembered as a master teacher and a mentor to generations of Hunter students. She was an early advocate of graduate education for women and a supporter of professional training for married women with children. In 1981, President Donna Shalala recognized Ruth's important contributions to Hunter College, awarding her an honorary doctorate, stating: "Ruth Weintraub created an 'old girls' network' before the phrase was coined." Ruth, like many Hunter graduates profiled in the following pages, saw a need and filled it.

At the time of Ruth's retirement, Blanche D. Blank, a former student who became a professor of political science at Hunter, and later acting president, described "the end of an era." Blank listed the ingredients of Ruth's era: creativity, invention, deep concern, careful follow-through, and moral courage. The ideas she pursued at Hunter—interdisciplinary programs, tutorials, administrative internships, legislative internships, urban studies, and accelerated BA-MA programs—were novel and important. As a teacher, Ruth was an inspiration to all who studied with her. Her classes were based on careful preparation, forceful presentation, and persistent Socratic-style prodding. She demanded and received excellence, encouraging her students to search for truth, to develop their critical faculties, and to be concerned with human freedom in the fullest sense.

In 1998, at a memorial service held for Ruth, another former student, Blanche Wiesen Cook, recapped the lasting influence she had on student activists: "For political Hunterites from the 1940s to her retirement, Ruth Weintraub was the mother of us all. A great chain of being extends from Bella Abzug and Mim Kelber, Hunter Student Council president and editor in 1941, to Florence Howe and Helene D. Goldfarb, presidents in 1950 and 1951, to my own year as president in 1961. Our lives have been linked by Ruth Weintraub who first taught us about politics and power, who encouraged our dedication to activism—as students, and public citizens."

Ruth Goldstein Weintraub was one of thousands of students who arrived at Hunter ready and eager to learn how to navigate in a world that offered them opportunities for professional development that had not been possible for their mothers. In the classrooms and clubs of the college they met students of different backgrounds who were, like themselves, academically serious and professionally ambitious. They met faculty who offered guidance in constructing a life of meaning. They encountered deans who were there to help them pursue their dreams.

Their dreams and their life stories were influenced by the changes in the standard of living and culture experienced by Americans in the period under consideration. The students of each period outlined below were also influenced by the accomplishments of the alumnae who preceded them.

Chapter One: *Mihi Cura Futuri* (1870–1920)

The college, which opened in 1870 as a combined high school and normal college, was the first public high school combined with the first full-time normal school for the girls of New York City. Before its establishment, girls who completed the eighth grade and wanted to become elementary school teachers could enroll in part-time pedagogical training programs. Thomas Hunter and his supporters rejected this approach to preparing teachers for the rapidly growing population of the city. The institution he envisaged had two unusual features. First, all girls who completed eighth grade in the city, specifically including Catholic, Jewish, and Black students, were invited to apply, and were accepted based on written examinations. Second, the school would provide a full liberal arts curriculum, as Hunter believed that teachers must have sufficient advanced learning to teach.

Students profiled in this chapter: Emma Requa, mathematics, 1870; Julia Richman, education, 1872; Helen Gray Cone, English, 1876; Margaret Barclay Wilson, biology, 1884; Edna Wells Luetz, art, 1915; E. Adelaide Hahn, classics, 1915; Mary Meade, classics, 1918.

Chapter Two: Excellence and Activism (1920–1929)

Hunter College celebrated its Golden Jubilee in 1920, having graduated twenty-five thousand students, most of whom became teachers in the public schools of the city. The culture of high achievement, established in the first decades of the college, was maintained by the students of the 1920s. These students added an activist dimension to college life by taking charge of student organizations. In this endeavor, they were supported by President George Samler Davis, Hunter's second president, who recognized the value of student clubs in encouraging initiative, developing responsibility, and emphasizing action to assure a more just future. In a demonstration of student activism, on January 5, 1927, the student newspaper carried a banner headline announcing, "Hunter World's Largest Woman's College Urgently Needs New Building, 12,146 Girls Campaign." The students explained that overcrowding had led to using annexes in Manhattan, Brooklyn, and Queens, which was economically wasteful.

Students profiled in this chapter: Mina Rees, mathematics, 1923; Bella Visono Dodd, history, 1925; Ruth Goldstein Weintraub, history, 1925; Edna Flannery Kelly, history, 1928; Marion Wilson Starling, classics, 1928.

Chapter Three: A Turbulent Decade (1929–1939)

James M. Kieran, a longtime member of the Hunter faculty and dean of education, was installed as Hunter's third president on March 26, 1929. In view of the continued rapid growth of the student body, which now included a day session with 5,500 students, an evening session of 7,772, and a summer session of 3,190, President Kieran reversed the policy of his predecessor and agreed to give up the building on Park Avenue in exchange for five buildings to be constructed on a planned campus in the Bronx. Students writing in the 1930 yearbook described the plan as "Utopia."

In 1933, Kieran announced his retirement. Eugene A. Colligan was installed as the fourth president of Hunter College on May 4, 1934. He was soon embroiled in controversy as he moved to put an end to Hunter's participation in the national student peace movement. The Student Council condemned his actions as a complete nullification of student self-government. Student mobilizations for peace continued. On February 14, 1936, the attention of all Hunter administrators, faculty, students, and alumnae turned to the four-alarm fire that destroyed the sixty-three-year-old main college building on Park Avenue.

Unlike his predecessor, President Colligan had no intention of giving up the original site of the college. He was joined by faculty, students, and alumnae in lobbying the Board of Higher Education to rebuild. Colligan addressed the citizens of New York on WMCA radio. In June 1939, having won the battle over the future of the Park Avenue campus, Colligan announced his retirement.

Students profiled in this chapter: Virginia Levitt Snitow, history, 1931; Sylvia Feldman Porter, economics, 1932; Pauli Murray, English, 1933; Belle (Bel) Kaufman, English, 1934; Soia Mentschikoff, political science, 1934; Lucy Schildkret Dawidowicz, English, 1936; Beatrice Brown, music, 1937; Gertrude Elion, chemistry, 1937, Lilian Rosovsky (Ross), English, 1939.

Chapter Four: War and Peace (1939–1949)

The World of Tomorrow, the World's Fair in Flushing, Queens, opened in April 1939. Hunter's contribution included a film starring students, *Hunter Prepares Women for the World of Tomorrow*. Several months later, on the college's seventieth birthday, February 14, 1940, Acting President George N. Shuster supervised the laying of the cornerstone of the new sixteen-story modern academic building at 695 Park Avenue. On September 1, Shuster was installed as Hunter's fifth president. *The New York Times* reported that invitations to eighteen hundred American colleges and universities, government officials, and organizations were sent to attend the dedication of the new building and the inauguration of President Shuster.

The new building, which was the only fireproof structure in the neighborhood, became the center of emergency preparedness drills following the attack on Pearl Harbor in December 1941. President Shuster chaired a defense committee of faculty trained to prepare for an air attack. The War Service Training Program at Hunter was adopted after weeks of review of military needs by a faculty committee. Hunter was the first civilian college in the nation to offer courses in cryptography and cryptanalytics. More than forty special courses were added to the Hunter curriculum during the war, among them nursing classes to meet the needs caused by the war.

In February 1943, the American Negro Culture course was added to the curriculum after years of pressure by the Toussaint L'Ouverture Society. In connection with the course, a shelf of books dealing with Black culture was added to the library. In 1946, Professor Mary Huff Diggs, a Phi Beta Kappa graduate with degrees from Bryn Mawr, the University of Minnesota, Fisk University, and the University of Pennsylvania, was hired as the first full-time Black tenure-track professor at Hunter.

President Shuster, sensing malaise among Hunter students, addressed them in the 1947 yearbook: "I understand completely how bewildered a young person must be when . . . she looks about in vain for something to do which has either intrinsic significance or relationship to the play as a whole. . . . It is not exaggerating your importance in the least to say that the decisive query of our time is not what happens to the atom bomb, but what happens to the college woman of America."

Students profiled in this chapter: Pearl Primus, biology, 1940; Ivy O. Roach Brooks, biology, 1940; Rosalyn Sussman Yalow, physics, 1941; Marjorie Henderson Ellis, biology, 1941; Ada Louise Landman Huxtable, art, 1941; Bella Savitsky Abzug, political science, 1942; Eugenie Clark, biology, 1942; Regina Resnik, music education, 1942; Ruby Wallace Dee, Romance languages, 1944; Anita Arrow Summers, economics, 1945; Elaine Small Klein, speech and theater, 1948.

Chapter Five: "A Natural Training Ground for Feminism" (1950–1964)

Throughout the decade, President Shuster spoke out for civil liberties and against government interference with academic freedom. Nevertheless, the Board of Higher Education suspended three Hunter faculty due to their membership in the Communist Party. Meryl Fialka, who graduated in 1954, wrote an opinion piece in the student newspaper questioning the right of the Board of Higher Education to fire professors based on their membership in the Communist Party, pointing out that it was a legal political party. Her response to McCarthyism was to declare: "Utilization of the tactics which we condemn in other societies cannot possibly strengthen any democratic institutions."

In 1957, *Mademoiselle* featured a profile of Hunter College as part of a series on outstanding colleges and universities. The author noted that Hunter students do not have to wait for a vacation trip to take advantage of New York's art museums, libraries, and operas. They have the city for their campus. The graduates of that year recognized the benefits of a Hunter education. They spoke of independence of thought, based on reason and understanding, on perception and cultivated intuition; they were aware of the importance of intellectual humility, ambition, service, and responsibility to the world community.

Students profiled in this chapter: Florence Rosenfeld Howe, English, 1950; Mildred Spiewak Dresselhaus, physics, 1951; Antonia Pantoja, sociology, 1952; Evelyn Sass Handler, biology, 1952; Rita Abrams Hauser, history, 1954; Martina Arroyo, Romance languages, 1956; Audre Lorde, English, 1959; Doris Derby, anthropology, 1961.

Chapter One

Mihi Cura Futuri (1870–1920)

In 1847, the New York State legislature established the Free Academy "for the purpose of extending the benefits of education gratuitously, to persons who have been pupils in the common [elementary] schools of the city and county of New York." The Free Academy, later renamed City College, accepted only boys. City leaders, concerned about providing teachers for the common schools, also recognized the need to educate girls beyond the eighth grade. In 1854, the legislature added a provision to the original act: "to continue the existing Free Academy and organize a similar institution for Females." Finally, on November 17, 1869, the New York Board of Education, twelve commissioners appointed by the mayor, established the Free Normal and High School, and appointed Thomas Hunter its first president.

Thomas Hunter was nineteen years old when he arrived in New York City in 1850. Forced to leave Ireland due to his strongly expressed democratic views, he found employment teaching drawing, reading, writing, and arithmetic, in Public School (P.S.) 35 on Thirteenth Street near Sixth Avenue. Seven years later he was promoted to principal of the school, the outstanding boys' school in the city at the time. Hunter became president of the Principals' Association and the head of the first free evening high school in the United States. He was keenly aware of the teacher shortage facing the public schools of the city, which enrolled one hundred thousand pupils, many of whom were the children of immigrants.

In 1870, New York City, which was then limited to Manhattan Island, was the most populous city in the United States with 942,292 residents. A decade later its population reached 1,206,299, and by 1890 an additional 500,000 people had settled in the city. In 1898, New York City was reorganized to include the five boroughs of Manhattan, Brooklyn, Queens, the Bronx, and Staten Island. The population of the city reached 3,437,202 in 1900. To meet the needs of its growing population, the city established transportation systems, housing, jobs, public schools, and cultural institutions.

Until the new school opened its doors, girls who completed the eighth grade and wanted to become teachers enrolled in part-time pedagogical training, segregated into white and colored classes, following the pattern of the elementary schools, which remained segregated in the city in the decades following the Civil War. Thomas Hunter rejected this approach to preparing teachers. The institution he created had two radical features. First, all girls who completed eighth grade in the city, including Catholic, Jewish, and Black students, were invited to apply, with acceptance based on a written examination. Students were examined anonymously. Each was given a number, and only that number was placed on her test paper. Hunter believed that this would ensure fairness for every candidate. Second, the school would provide a full liberal arts curriculum as well as pedagogical training, as Hunter believed that teachers should have sufficient advanced knowledge to teach effectively.

Over one thousand students applied for admission on the second floor of a rented loft building on Fourth Street and Broadway when the school opened on Valentine's Day 1870. The size of the student body made this college different from the 30–40 women's colleges offering degrees at the time, the majority of which had fifty students or fewer. Only Vassar had more than two hundred students registered. The seven hundred girls who were admitted were divided into three groups based on their educational attainments. It is unknown if there were any Catholic or Black students admitted in 1870. At least one Jewish student, Julia Richman, was in the group. By 1873, there is evidence of nine Black students attending the college. *Scientific American* in December 1874 reported: "The college has an attendance of over 1,000 students, from all parts of the city, and all creeds, classes, and nationalities."

The board also appointed Lydia Wadleigh, the principal of P.S. 47, the first-ranked public school for girls, as "lady superintendent," and assigned ten of the best vice-principals, all experienced teachers in the city schools, to teach in the new school. From the beginning, the rented space was inadequate as the ground floor housed a carriage shop and the third floor was used as an armory. Students complained of bad odors and unwanted interest from men in uniform. Within a few months, the City of New York granted the new school an uptown plot of land, bounded by Park and Lexington Avenues, Sixty-Eighth and Sixty-Ninth Streets, on which to build a permanent building. The Board of Education hired an architect.

President Hunter's plan to prepare teachers for the city was revolutionary, as it was based on providing higher education in a variety of subjects to girls. Other normal schools offered teaching methodology without teaching advanced subject matter. As an experienced teacher and principal, Hunter was convinced that elementary school teachers needed more knowledge of the subjects they would teach. To that end, he established a liberal arts program as the centerpiece of the curriculum of the new school. Latin, history, mathematics, natural and physical sciences, modern languages (including English), music, drawing, and philosophy were included. He planned to support pedagogical training in a model elementary school, the Normal College Training Department (NCTD, later, the Model School), for practice teaching.

In the first months of operation, Hunter addressed the pressing needs of his new school. To avoid confusion, he secured a name change for the school, which was officially renamed the Normal College of the City of New York by the state legislature on April 6, 1870. President Hunter added to the small staff provided by the Board of Education, hiring a vice president, Arthur Henry Dundon, a principal in the Jersey City school system. Dundon, a Latinist, recommended a line from Ovid's *Metamorphoses*, *Mihi cura futuri*, "the care of the future is mine," for the school motto. Hunter asked Superintendent Lydia Wadleigh to serve temporarily as principal of the NCTD, which would provide classroom teaching experience under the supervision of qualified teachers for Normal College students. The NCTD opened near the college on Saint Marks Place in September 1870. It included the first public kindergarten in the city.

During its first year of operation, President Hunter, who was also professor of intellectual philosophy, taught philosophy and the theory and practice of teaching; Vice President Dundon, who was also professor of English and Latin, taught English language and Latin. Hunter hired two additional professors: Joseph Anthony Gillet to teach mathematics and physics, and Charles Albert Schlegel to teach German and French. Two tutors, George Mangold and Charlotte V. Hutchings, were hired to teach music and chorus.

On July 12, 1870, only five months after the opening of the Normal College, the first commencement was held at the Academy of Music, the most popular auditorium in New York City. Ninety-seven young women, judged to be ready to teach, graduated and were added to the supply of available teachers for the city's elementary schools. President Hunter selected five of the best graduates for the staff of the NCTD, including Emma M. Requa, who had studied mathematics and would later become a member of the college faculty and the chairman of its math department.

Emma Requa remained closely connected with her alma mater for decades. Born in 1852 in New York City, to Elijah Lee Requa and Mary Ann Cramsey Requa, Emma was one of five children. She attended the Twelfth Street School, Miss Wadleigh's school, with her older sister, Mary

Figure 1.1. Professor Emma Requa, chairman, Department of Mathematics, 1914. *Source*: Archives and Special Collections, Hunter College Libraries, Hunter College of the City University of New York, New York City.

Augusta; both girls were members of the first class of the Normal College. Their professional development, sketched below, is exemplary of a group of students who later helped to shape the culture of the college.

At first, Emma taught in the NCTD and later in the Normal College, where she was assigned a variety of subjects: gymnastics, history, and English. Ultimately, she was transferred to the Department of Mathematics and Physics. In recognition of her deep knowledge of mathematics, Emma was granted a bachelor of science degree at the twenty-ninth commencement of the college in June 1898. Nearly a decade later, when mathematics became an independent department, she was named professor and chairman of the Department of Mathematics.

Emma Requa was successful in attracting to her department large numbers of brilliant students. She established a Mathematics Club in 1908 to engage students in original research. One of her students, Louisa M. Webster, who later became a member of the department, published an article in 1917 about the importance of such clubs. She explained that the club was a response to the desire of both the teaching and student bodies to study the phases of mathematical development that were not covered in regular classes. She added, "It aims to be a source of profitable pleasure."

Meetings were held once a month from October to June. The graduates of the Mathematics Department were welcome to attend regular meetings. Many attended and others sent reports about their professional experiences, which were helpful to undergraduates. Professor Requa addressed each meeting, suggesting research or commenting on an item in the news. Faculty and students volunteered to present papers, often speaking without notes, using a model or the blackboard to illustrate their comments. Topics presented by student members included "The Mysticism of Numbers," "The History of Japanese Mathematics," "What Women Have Accomplished in Science," "Mathematical Fallacies," and "The History of Time Pieces."

Student leadership was an important part of the culture of the club. A president, vice-president, and secretary were chosen from a pool of sophomores and juniors whose scholarship was superior, while the treasurer was a faculty member who collected the fifty-cent dues and advised on expenditures. Webster reported that former presidents did especially well following graduation. One was teaching in elementary school, two in high school, two had temporary college appointments, one was in medical school, and one was studying law. She also noted that, within the past three years, eighteen of the department's graduates had received master's degrees. In a demonstration of their continuing connection with the mathematics department at Normal College, several who had pursued graduate studies together presented the department with a set of books they had found especially useful, as an expression of appreciation of the benefit they derived from the club.

Emma Requa understood the importance of giving undergraduates opportunities to come into repeated contact with graduate students and faculty who were involved in research. She encouraged her faculty to hold regular discussions with students outside of the classroom, allowing students to express their ideas and to test their theories in an atmosphere that encouraged their professional aspirations and that celebrated their accomplishments. She took great interest in student plans following graduation, suggesting that some pursue advanced degrees in mathematics. She informed others when special courses were to be offered at universities or other academic sites. She notified them when examinations were to be held for teaching positions, even for those in other cities.

Emma and her sister, Mary Augusta, lived with their widowed mother until her death in 1908. Both sisters, graduates of 1870, were among the founders of the Associate Alumnae in 1872, an organization of former Normal College students who attended annual reunions at the college, marveling at the development of the college facilities, the faculty, and the students. The Associate Alumnae made important contributions to creating a culture of excellence and activism at the college. Among their early contributions were books to begin a library and a plan to create a settlement house near the college where students could volunteer. Emma Requa demonstrated awareness of the importance of collegiality in an additional way, becoming one of the organizers of the Faculty Club, serving as its second president. She established the custom of enjoying afternoon tea to promote good fellowship among the growing faculty.

Following the first graduation in 1870, additional faculty were hired. Philip M. W. Redfield was appointed professor of natural science; fourteen tutors in mathematics, French, and music, including many women, were added to the teaching staff. In the early years all the professors in the college were men who had completed the PhD. The tutors were primarily women and a small number of men who had not received doctoral degrees.

The architect hired by the Board of Education to design the permanent home for the college on Park Avenue was fired when his efforts displeased the board. President Hunter was asked to try his hand at the assignment. The board quickly approved his design; work commenced on the building in the spring of 1871. Construction was delayed for several months due to a bricklayers' strike. The building cost $1 million, three times the original commitment from the board.

The new red brick building, a four-story Gothic style edifice, was ready for the opening of classes on September 1, 1873. Helen Gray Cone, a fourteen-year-old new student who, like Emma Requa, would become a beloved faculty member and later chairman of the English Department, was in the first class to enter the new building. She described her experience: "Goats roamed around the barren neighborhood. . . . There were vacant lots from Fifth to Third Avenues, with . . . only one real house in the near vicinity, and the only sidewalk, that around the College building. But to the girls of 1873 our . . . building was . . . spacious and magnificent."

The new facility contained thirty recitation rooms, two large lecture rooms, an art studio, a physics demonstration laboratory, a chapel seating two thousand, a storage room for textbooks, a wide hallway called the calisthenium (a place where calisthenics are performed) for exercise, a janitor's apartment, and a basement. There was no cafeteria; students ate sandwiches brought from home or bought cookies from the janitor in classrooms. Illumination came from open gas flames as there were no electric lights. There were no telephones, no typewriters, no clerks. At the time of its opening, the college building served a student body of about fourteen hundred girls, while the NCTD served six hundred pupils. A three-story red brick structure was added to the eastern end of the property on Lexington Avenue to serve their needs.

The neighborhood around the new college building developed rapidly as churches, synagogues, hospitals, the Seventh Regiment Armory, a police station, and a firehouse were built nearby. The Union Theological Seminary, erected on Park Avenue between Sixty-Ninth and Seventieth Streets, and the American Museum of Natural History, which resided at the Central Park Arsenal on Sixty-Fourth Street and Fifth Avenue until its permanent building opened on Central Park West in 1877, were the only neighboring educational institutions. The Metropolitan Museum of Art moved nearby to Fifth Avenue and Eighty-Second Street in 1880. The Third Avenue El, connecting passengers from South Ferry to 129th Street, opened on December 30, 1878. The Second Avenue El was completed in August 1880. Brownstone houses were built on the side streets that connected the avenues.

Mimi Scherzinger, who graduated in 1878, reported walking with thirty of her classmates from P.S. 53 on East Seventy-Ninth Street to the

Normal College to take the entrance exams. Sixty-six years later, Scherzinger looked back at her time at the college: "Three happy years were passed in this fine educational institution, with wonderful Thomas Hunter as the President, an austere, but friendly Lydia Wadleigh, as the dean, and the five dignified members of the faculty are all a part of a pleasing looking-backward picture of our Normal College days. Then graduation day, with our well-earned diplomas. In June 1878, we reluctantly said good-bye to our beautiful red-brick college, with the lavender wisteria vines clambering up the walls, and the gardens just beginning to grow up to help beautify the surroundings."

In December 1879, *Harper's New Monthly* carried a long article that provided additional details about the Normal College. The journalist began with a description of the daily chapel service, a feature of most colleges of the period. On the platform were the professors and tutors. At five minutes to nine a woman seated at the piano began to play a lively march and 1,542 students filed in silently. They stood in front of their seats until all were in their places when a signal from the pianist indicated the time to sit. William Wood, chairman of the Board of Education, read a chapter from the Bible; a nonsectarian hymn was sung to the accompaniment of the organ. *Harper's* estimated that there were two hundred Jewish girls among the 1,542 students enrolled.

President Hunter periodically invited prominent guests to address the student body. The Visitors' Book included General Ulysses S. Grant, General William Tecumseh Sherman, Dom Pedro (emperor of Brazil), Liliuokalani (queen of the Hawaiian Kingdom), and Eulalia (infanta of Spain). There followed the opportunity for individual students to recite a selection from memory. Among the offerings on the day when the journalist from *Harper's* visited were a quotation from Shakespeare's *As You Like It*, a maxim by François de La Rochefoucauld offered in French, and a passage about knowledge by Thomas Henry Huxley.

At the end of the session, some students remained in the hall for their music class, others went to their assigned classrooms, while others went to the calisthenium. President Hunter required daily exercise in groups of three hundred for fifteen minutes. Each student was provided with a strong elastic band, with wooden handles, which they stretched from side to side, from shoulder to hip, from back to breast, and from over the head to chin, in ways designed to develop muscular strength. At 9:50, all students were in their classrooms, where they would remain until the end of the day. There were four periods a day, each of fifty minutes, with intervals of five minutes during which students were permitted to converse, and thirty minutes for lunch. Professors and tutors moved from room to room at the end of each period.

The curriculum established by President Hunter was demanding, reflecting his commitment to a liberal arts education. It included three years of Latin; two years of history—ancient and modern; three years of French or German; three years of English—composition, rhetoric, and literature; three years of math—algebra and geometry; three years of a variety of science classes—physics, chemistry, astronomy, geology, botany, and zoology; and classes in music, drawing, and penmanship. In their third year, students practiced teaching in the NCTD. There were opportunities to teach in the kindergarten and primary school (grades 1–4), which enrolled boys and girls, or in the grammar school (grades 5–8), which enrolled only girls.

In 1879, the original three-year course was extended to four years, in recognition of the fact that more time was needed to adequately teach the subjects in the curriculum. In 1888, New York State recognized the Normal College as a distinct corporate body with its own Board of Trustees, composed of members of the Board of Education and the president of the college. The college was granted an annual appropriation of $125,000, equal to the appropriation for the College of the City of New York (CCNY, formerly, Free Academy). Normal College began to offer two courses of study: a four-year Normal course for those planning to teach and a five-year academic course for those preferring a general education. By 1903, all students were required to study for seven years, with the first four years legally separated and accredited by the Board of Regents as the Normal College High School. By 1908, Normal College offered qualified high school graduates a four-year academic course with a fully accredited bachelor of arts degree.

While the curriculum developed, the diverse background of the students remained. In 1879 a delegation of Normal College students was selected to welcome President Benjamin Harrison to New York City to mark the Centennial Celebration of the Constitution of the United States. Two Black students were among the delegates selected to throw flower petals in his path. Anne Alida Abrahams, a Jewish student, was chosen to deliver the Address of Welcome to the City. In 1886, President Hunter proudly listed the occupations of the parents of Normal College students to demonstrate their diversity: bankers, day laborers, presidents, coachmen, clergymen, masons, physicians, bookkeepers, blacksmiths, clothiers, carpenters, lawyers, brokers, clerks, teachers, office-holders (city, state, and federal), widows, traders, editors, journalists, reporters, janitors, grocers, and horse dealers.

Growing demand for admission to the Normal College led to higher enrollment and within a decade after the inauguration of the new building on Sixty-Eighth Street, the college had become crowded. By 1884, a restriction was placed on the number of admissions to the college. From 1880 to 1890 enrollment increased from 2,191 to 2,746; in 1900, enrollment climbed to 3,871. Finally, in 1910, with the removal of the high school division from the building, enrollment on Sixty-Eighth Street temporarily returned to a more manageable 1,244. As enrollment for the Normal College continued to grow, annexes in various parts of the city were rented to accommodate student growth.

The Associate Alumnae, imbued with the spirit of the motto of their alma mater, *Mihi cura futuri,* volunteered to support the efforts of President Hunter and in so doing began to influence the culture of Normal College. In its early years, the Alumnae focused on support for the free kindergarten movement, created a loan fund for needy students, started the college library, and established an alumnae newsletter. Eleonore Funk (Mrs. Otto Hahn), of the class of 1875, edited the monthly newsletter, *Alumnae News*, for fifty years, informing the growing numbers of alumnae of the activities of their association.

In 1894, the Normal College Alumnae House was established at 446 East Seventy-Second Street. The annual report for the house in 1911 explained: "The Normal College Alumnae House exists for the mutual benefit of its neighbors and the students and graduates of the Normal College. Its purpose is to give social expression to democracy; so to study its neighborhood as to gain insight into its best life and its special needs, and as a result of the study to stimulate self-help and cooperation, and wisely to lead and share the movement of the neighborhood toward civic consciousness and righteousness." This project, funded by alumnae and staffed by alumnae and students, was incorporated in 1912 as the Lenox Hill Settlement Association and reincorporated in 1922 as the Lenox Hill Neighborhood Association.

The alumnae also began to hold annual reunions. At their gathering in 1885, Eva B. Hickinbottom, sister of future dean Annie Hickinbottom, demonstrated the continued commitment of the alumnae to Normal College, as well as a new spirit of independence. She asked rhetorically, "How many of us would be delighted to have women as members of the

Board of Education; to have a member of our own Alumnae elected by our Association to present us to the Committee on Normal College! Do you think it an impossibility? The Associate Alumnae of Vassar (founded in 1871) are working for this very thing." Another alumna asked: "Does it ever occur to any one of us that in this college for women there is not a single woman professor? What a humiliating spectacle for us to contemplate."

The graduates of the 1870s and 1880s included serious and determined women: Jennie Merrill and Ida Conant (both with PhDs) in kindergarten and elementary education, Julia Richman and Katherine Devereux Blake in educational administration, Emma Requa and Helen Gray Cone who became department heads in the Normal College, Dr. Mary Augusta Requa (sister of Emma Requa) and Dr. Margaret Barclay Wilson in medicine and hygiene, Mary A. Wells in social work, Harriet Keith in vocational placement, and Annie Hickinbottom in counseling. These women and scores of Normal College tutors and some New York City teachers and administrators formed a small, mostly unmarried group whose professional and personal lives were shaped by their ties to the Normal College. This generation of graduates was deeply motivated to do something important with their lives. They advocated changes in the Normal College curriculum to match curricular opportunities available at Vassar, established in 1865, and at the more recently established Barnard, founded in 1889. They embraced the twin ideals of acquiring a broad-based liberal arts education and the concept of service, to the school, to the community, and to other women.

A close look at the life of one such alumna, Julia Richman, who graduated in 1872, provides an opportunity to know more about the private and professional lives of this generation of Normal College graduates. Born in the Chelsea district of Manhattan in 1855 to Moses and Theresa Richman, Jewish immigrants from Prague, Julia was the third of five children. Until she was five years old, the family lived in an upscale apartment at 150 Seventh Avenue. For the next six years they lived in bucolic Huntington, Long Island, where they were the only Jewish family. Missing the Jewish community of New York City, the family returned to the city where Julia's sisters married, and her brother joined their father in business.

Julia chose a different path. While still a young girl she declared, "I am not pretty . . . and I am not going to marry, but before I die all New York will know my name!" She announced her intention to become a teacher, a decision vehemently opposed by her father who insisted that Julia follow the conventional matrimonial path taken by her sisters. With great tenacity, Julia convinced her parents to allow her to pursue secondary education. In 1870, fifteen-year-old Julia Richman enrolled in the Normal College. She completed the rigorous three-year course of study described above. She also studied innovative methods of instructional pedagogy and taught in the NCTD.

Richman ranked fourth in her graduating class. She was seventeen years old when she was hired to teach in P.S. 59 on Fifty-Seventh Street and Second Avenue, then considered part of the Lower East Side. As in many of the city's schools, classes were separated by gender. Classes were large, holding up to fifty pupils. Non-English-proficient students were placed in entry-level grades regardless of their age until they mastered enough English to be moved into upper grades. Julia had trouble with her

Figure 1.2. Julia Richman, 1888. *Source*: Archives and Special Collections, Hunter College Libraries, Hunter College of the City University of New York, New York City.

first class of twelve-year-old boys. After two years she was transferred to the girls' division of P.S. 59 where she remained for seven years, winning a reputation as a gifted teacher.

Richman's father died in 1875. Mores of the time forbade an unmarried woman teacher to live alone; hence, Julia lived with her widowed mother for the next twenty-six years. The arrangement worked well as Julia's mother did all the cooking, cleaning, and laundry while Julia devoted her time to teaching and volunteer work. She conducted Sabbath School classes at her synagogue, the Reform Temple Ahawath Chesed. She was also a founder of the Young Ladies Charitable Union, which organized social events to raise money for the poor. The union became incorporated into the Hebrew Free School Association, a prominent educational agency on the Lower East Side. The association established a settlement house that offered immigrants free hot meals, used clothing, basic literacy skills, and religious instruction. In her volunteer work as well as in her professional work Julia demonstrated the influence of the college motto as well as strong leadership skills.

In 1882, Julia was appointed vice principal of Grammar School 13 (grades 4–6), located at Forty-Sixth Street and Second Avenue. Two years later, at the age of twenty-nine, she was promoted to the position of principal of the girls' division of P.S. 77 on York Avenue and Eighty-Fifth Street. Richman was the first Normal College graduate, the first person of Jewish descent, and the youngest person to be selected as a principal of a public school in Manhattan. She worked there for nineteen years, developing innovative educational approaches for immigrant children. She established an English immersion program that incorporated American history and civics along with basic literacy skills.

Richman's programs were based on her personal experience as a teacher of immigrant children. One of her innovations was to group students homogeneously by level of ability: high, average, and below average. Significantly, she placed her most experienced teachers in charge of classes of below average learners, convinced that those students had the greatest need. She recognized that these students lost their fear of failure when surrounded by others functioning at the same level. Brighter students, she theorized, would be stimulated by interaction with their peers and had less need for the best teachers. She also tried a system of flexible promotions where students were promoted whenever they demonstrated a mastery of the material. A third innovation was her campaign to encourage greater involvement by parents. She organized a lecture series for mothers offering information about hygiene. She formed a mothers' club that met on Thursday afternoons to listen to speakers, discuss books, and listen to classical music. She invited participation of the fathers in a highly popular athletic program for boys. Under her leadership, this program evolved into the Public Schools Athletic League.

In 1897, determined to update her professional skills, Richman enrolled in graduate courses at NYU's School of Pedagogy. In 1903, she again made history when she was appointed district superintendent for the Lower East Side, the first woman to be so honored. Her district was still predominantly an immigrant neighborhood. It included fourteen day and evening schools, twenty-three thousand students, and six hundred teachers. She personified the mottos of both of her alma maters: "Care of the future is mine" and "To persevere and to excel." Her immediate supervisor, Superintendent William Maxwell, described her as an excellent executive, innovative and creative. Subordinates found her assertive, exacting, and tenacious. Students loved her maternal qualities.

As district superintendent, Richman continued to innovate. She advocated English-language immersion strategies, programs in hygiene and culture, and vocational training. She also pioneered programs to provide educational opportunities for her district's handicapped students. She divided this group to the best of her understanding into two categories: those with severe problems including blindness, deafness, mutism, lameness, and mental retardation, and those with fewer needs including impaired vision, moderate hearing loss, asthma, heart problems, or emotional disturbances. She established fourteen specialized classes offering modified curricula to respond to the unique needs of these pupils. These classes were the forerunners of modern-day special education programs.

Richman also created a program for students who were frequently delinquent or truant. These students disrupted classes, committed crimes on school property, and had a negative influence on younger students. They were typically expelled or sent to reformatories. Public School 120 opened in October 1905 offering programs to 135 boys, judged to be hardened liars, gamblers, and pickpockets. The teaching staff included six women and five men with special training in psychology who had volunteered for the assignment. The school offered small class sizes, two teachers to each classroom, and a collaborative learning environment. In addition, it had an extensive athletic program with emphasis on sportsmanship and obeying the rules of the game. The teachers were pleased when 49 percent of the students succeeded.

In June 1912, Julia sailed to France for a much-needed summer vacation. On board, she experienced an attack of appendicitis and died in Paris on June 24. Her body was returned to New York City for burial. On the day of her funeral, July 8, the New York City Board of Education ordered the flags of all the public schools to be flown at half-mast in her honor. In 1923, a new public high school was opened on the Upper East Side of Manhattan on E. Sixty-Seventh Street between Second and First Avenues; it was named the Julia Richman School.

It wasn't only the alumnae, like Richman, who began to influence the culture of the college. In the 1880s student clubs were established at Normal College, which allowed students to pursue their interests in a variety of areas. These clubs began to have an influence on the life of the college. The two oldest clubs were the Philomathean Society, which promoted friendly relations among students, and the Alpha Beta Gamma Society, which founded a double choral quartet to entertain at college events. Soon, a branch of the Agassiz Association, dedicated to natural science, became active on campus.

Figure 1.3. Alpha Beta Gamma Society, 1903. *Source*: Archives and Special Collections, Hunter College Libraries, Hunter College of the City University of New York, New York City.

The Phoebean Literary Society was added to these opportunities for informal education. Bird, botany, dramatic, and mandolin clubs were formed. Student debates became popular. A student council room was established on the top floor of the building to provide space for leaders of these groups and clubs to meet after classes, which ended daily at 2 p.m.

President Hunter viewed the success of the Normal School through the lens of its admissions policy, writing in 1888: "In no other country in the world—not even in any other republic—could the rich and poor meet together in the same recitation rooms on terms of perfect equality. The far-reaching influence for the State of this commingling of classes and races is something that might well attract the attention of the statesman, for it tends, more than anything else, to make a homogeneous American nation." Several years later, a student expressed a similar sentiment: "The great thing which we Americans have to be thankful for is not the education of the poor, but the mingling in thought and feeling of all classes; it is this that is the safeguard of the Republic." Her comment, penned in 1891, is an indication that some students were aware of the significance of the Normal College experience.

In 1889 the first student journal of the college, the *Echo*, was established. Named for the talkative woodland nymph in Ovid's myth of "Echo and Narcissus," Echo, spurned by Narcissus, retreated to a cave where she became a voice heard by all. Short stories, poems, and articles written and edited by successive groups of students continued to appear for more than fifty years. In the 1891 issue, a paean to Central Park captures the prose style and sentiments of Normal College students: "What is more distinctly American in our city than Central Park? Its ample grounds, its unstinted luxuriance, its alternation between primeval grandeur and the cultivation of today, its half-natural, half-artificial spots of verdure, are they not typical of our country?" The 1900 issue of the *Echo* listed fourteen clubs and an athletic program, including bowling, tennis, and basketball, which became the most popular sport. At the turn of the century the basketball team, the "Normal Five," played in Staten Island, New Paltz, New York, and Northampton, Massachusetts. Students of different classes, races, and religions not only took classes together; they also worked side by side in clubs, athletic events, and publications. The editors of the *Echo* started publishing annual graduation yearbooks in 1896. They changed the name and the format of the yearbook in 1902, calling it the *Wistarion*, in appreciation for the flowering wisteria vines that covered the Park Avenue side of the college building. The yearbook facilitated continuing contact among graduates as it included photos and home addresses.

Figure 1.4. Normal College Basketball, 1918. *Source*: Archives and Special Collections, Hunter College Libraries, Hunter College of the City University of New York, New York City.

As the student body grew, more faculty were hired to staff the departments that were established. Some were men with European doctorates, and many of the women were graduates of Normal College. Isidor Keller became chairman of the German Department. Eugene Aubert was appointed professor of French. Claudine Gray, one of Aubert's students, would later become chairman of the department. The faculty began to play a larger role in curriculum planning and in supporting student activities. With the death of Professor Dundon in 1899, President Hunter separated the English and Latin Departments that Dundon had chaired. George Meason Whicher was appointed chairman of Latin while Helen Gray Cone, a graduate of the college, was appointed chairman of the English

Department. Cone was the first graduate of the college to be appointed a department chairman. Like Emma Requa, who was appointed chairman of mathematics in 1908, Cone had an enduring influence on the culture of the college.

Helen Gray Cone was born on March 8, 1859, in Manhattan to Julia Gray and John Carpenter Cone. Her early childhood was spent in the fragrant woodlands surrounding the family home in Englewood, New Jersey. When Helen was six, the family returned to Manhattan. She was drawn to the poetry of Sir Walter Scott and Henry Wadsworth Longfellow, which her mother read to her, and she soon began penning her own verses. In 1870 she began to attend the grammar school on East 125th Street. Helen's teacher, Miss Granger, lent her books and encouraged her writing. Several of her poems were published in a children's magazine, *Our*

Figure 1.5. Professor Helen Gray Cone, chairman, Department of English, 1910. *Source*: Archives and Special Collections, Hunter College Libraries, Hunter College of the City University of New York, New York City.

Young Folks. In 1873, Helen entered the Normal College. She contributed a song, "The Good Ship Alma Mater," which became the commencement song at the college for many decades.

Following her graduation in 1876, Helen continued to write, publishing numerous poems, and to participate in the Associate Alumnae, which elected her president in 1886. She served for two years and remained a strong supporter of the group for the rest of her life. In 1889, she was hired by the college as a tutor and taught for a decade, again continuing to write and publish. In 1899, when she was appointed chairman of the English Department, she was simultaneously given the title professor, making her the first woman professor at the college.

Helen Gray Cone led the direction and growth of the English Department until her retirement in 1926. In 1911, she wrote a long letter to Hunter's new president, George Samler Davis, comparing the curriculum of the English Department at Wellesley to that at the Normal College and requesting more resources to hire faculty to better serve her students. During her long tenure, English classes in composition and literature were required for all students. Later classes in vocal expression were added to departmental offerings. English Department faculty served as advisors to the college publications, to the Shakespeare Society, and to the Journalism Club. In 1922, Cone recommended the establishment of an independent Department of Speech and Dramatics.

Professor Cone died in March 1934. The *Bulletin* printed a special issue to memorialize her passing. Colleagues, students, alumnae, and trustees contributed their thoughts about her extraordinary contributions to the college. Ruth Lewinson, a lawyer and alumna who graduated with Cone in 1876, was a member of the Board of Higher Education; she affirmed that Helen Gray Cone was the first to bring international reputation to the college through her poetic writings. She also inspired thousands of students and brought warmth and joy to her friends. Soia Mentschikoff, president of the Student Council in 1934, saw Cone as the incarnation of the college spirit. Soia credited her with engendering in the hearts of all its graduates the same reverence and love for the college that was part of her being. She declared that the student body joined hands with all who mourned the loss of Helen Gray Cone.

Professor Henrietta Prentiss, who became chairman of the Speech Department, reflected on another aspect of the importance of Professor Cone to the college community. She described Cone as "a gallant soul, high-minded, valiant in the defense of causes which were dear to her, wise in her handling of difficult situations." After Prentiss became chairman of the Speech Department, she added: "Her courage was contagious and her good sense a support. Inspired by her our graduates have been sent forth to demonstrate to countless young people how high and searching an adventure it is to think on those things which are lovely . . . and which are true."

Elizabeth P. Stein, assistant professor of English, advised the Shakespeare Society. She noted that following her retirement, Professor Cone, a recognized Shakespearian scholar, became the first honorary member of the Shakespeare Society. When the Shakespeare Society presented its first play, *King Lear*, in 1931, Cone wrote to the student members: "It gives me much pleasure to know that you are supplementing your classroom study by *living in* the plays of Shakespeare, through the attempt to render them in action. Nothing could add more to your power of appreciation or store your memories with greater riches." Stein's appreciation demonstrates Cone's continuing involvement with students and colleagues following her retirement.

Like Helen Gray Cone, Margaret Barclay Wilson, valedictorian of the class of 1884, was professionally associated with the college for half a century. Born in Dunfermline, Scotland, in 1863, she arrived in New York with her family at the age of seven. At her graduation, the prize-winning student was introduced by William Wood, chairman of the Board of Trustees, to Andrew Carnegie who hailed from the same Scottish town and was impressed by the scholastic achievements of the young woman. Wilson and Carnegie corresponded for many years. After his death in 1915, she privately published a book of excerpts from his speeches and addresses, *The Carnegie Anthology*.

Following graduation, Wilson taught for three years in an elementary school. She began her teaching career in the college in 1887 as a tutor in the Department of Biology. To prepare herself to teach physiology, she enrolled in the Women's Medical College of New York, obtaining an MD in 1893. Her medical training enabled her to convince the Hunter administration of the importance of establishing an independent Department of Physiology and Hygiene. She advanced through the ranks of instructor to associate and later professor and was named chairman of the department. Professor Wilson was also appointed honorary librarian for the college, serving from 1915 to 1928. Her successor in this role, Professor Joseph J. Reilly, described her contribution: "She had vision, reliance, and faith in Hunter's present and future."

Professor Wilson became internationally known as an authority on nutrition, food chemistry, and unusual foods. International visitors found their way to her laboratory to ask advice and to view her collection of books and food specimens, which she kept on display. During World War I, when England faced a serious food shortage, she was asked by the British Food Commission to come to London to review the situation and make recommendations to Parliament. Her report led to changes in the utilization of different flours for breadmaking that helped solve the shortage.

In 1917, the US Department of Health used her knowledge of food economy to prepare daily bulletins for the American public. In New York City, she lectured weekly to a group of two hundred nurses from city hospitals about nutrition and food economy during wartime. During the flu epidemic in 1918, she prepared large quantities of nutritious soup, which she personally distributed to families in need. She also helped organize students to work as nurse's aides to assist with the care of the sick in sections of the city where the need was great.

In 1929, Wilson donated her extensive collection of more than four thousand works on food, cookery, and nutrition in over thirty languages, including references dating back several centuries, to the New York Academy of Medicine. The following year she presented to the Academy a ninth-century manuscript of *Apicius*, the oldest known copy of the ancient book on cookery. She presented her collection of art, gems, ivories, textiles, and vases to Johns Hopkins University to establish a Museum of Decorative Arts. At the June 1945 commencement, President Shuster conferred an honorary doctor of science degree on Professor Wilson, praising her pioneering role in the teaching of physiology, hygiene, and dietetics, and recognizing that she "lighted the way for women to study medicine." Wilson died on October 6, 1945.

In 1895, on the twenty-fifth anniversary of the Normal College, *The New York Press* reported that three thousand of the four thousand New York City teachers were graduates of the college. The following year, the college reported having graduated 6,782 students, five thousand of whom had taught in the public schools. In 1898, following the unification of the outer boroughs and Manhattan, all the public schools of the city were placed under the leadership of Superintendent William Henry Maxwell. The new superintendent sought to control the supply and quality of public-school teachers, through new examinations, soon called "Maxwells." He established a public high school division that included schools for girls, expanding the number of students likely to apply to Normal College. He also created the New York Training School for Teachers (later Teachers College), eliminating the monopoly held by Normal College to educate the future teachers of New York City. Thomas Hunter responded to these changes in stages by expanding the offerings of the academic course and reducing the role of the normal course, making it a department within the academic course.

In 1894, *The New York Times* had reported that the college was adding to its original goals and that it was now prepared to provide opportunities for students who wished to enter the fields of medicine, law, journalism, and commerce. By 1902, the success of the Normal College in creating a quality liberal arts curriculum was recognized when it received full accreditation by the state Board of Regents. Accreditation of all Normal College degrees and programs made graduates of the college eligible for some of the graduate programs at Columbia University and NYU.

E. Adelaide Hahn was one of many who benefited from this development. In September 1907, Hahn graduated from the NCTD with high marks. She was surprised that she had not been required to take the admission test to attend Normal College High School, as she was among the best graduates of the NCTD. Due to a clerical error, she had not been informed to report for the first day of high school. When she learned that classes were starting, she raced to the building on Park Avenue and approached Annie E. Hickinbottom, the lady superintendent soon to be named dean, who reassured her: "So you're one of those poor young ones that didn't get notified." She helped Adelaide to find her place in the high school from which she graduated at the top of her class four years later. A study of Adelaide Hahn's life and career illustrates the character of a new generation of talented and determined Normal College students.

Hahn was born in New York in April 1893, the daughter of Otto Hahn, a native of Austria, and of Eleonore Funk Hahn, a graduate of the Normal College in 1875. Adelaide Hahn was homeschooled by her mother until the age of thirteen when she entered the NCTD for one year to prepare her for Normal College High School. Hahn continued her path as an excellent student, graduating first in her class in 1915, from Hunter College (formerly Normal College). Her majors were Latin, Greek, and French. She took graduate courses at Columbia, receiving an MA in classics in 1917 and a PhD in 1929. From 1917 to 1921 she was hired as an instructor in French at Hunter College. She joined the classics faculty in 1921 and was promoted to assistant professor in 1925, to

Figure 1.6. E. Adelaide Hahn, front row center, with *Bulletin* staff, 1917. *Source*: Archives and Special Collections, Hunter College Libraries, Hunter College of the City University of New York, New York City.

associate professor in 1933, and to professor in 1936, at which time she also became department chair. Professor Hahn chaired the department for twenty-seven years until her retirement in 1963.

Adelaide Hahn, like Helen Gray Cone and Emma Requa, was much more than a faculty member. She was a part of the life of the college; she succeeded her mother as editor of the *Alumnae News* in 1944 and continued in that post until she was elected president of the Alumnae Association in 1958, serving until 1962. Like Cone, whose poetry was published widely, Hahn achieved a significant reputation for her numerous scholarly publications in the field of comparative linguistics. Between 1920 and 1967 she published more than seventy-five articles in major academic journals. She published her dissertation, two monographs, and many popular pieces that appeared in the *New York Herald Tribune* and in *The World*. She was the first woman to hold the Collitz Professorship at the Linguistic Institute of the University of California at Berkeley, the first woman president of the Linguistic Society of America, and first woman vice president of the American Oriental Institute. At Hunter, her exuberant personality was on permanent display in the large, feathered hats she wore regularly. Professor Hahn died in 1967.

Having set the direction of the Normal College since its inception, President Hunter announced his plan to retire in September 1903. Professor Joseph Gillet, a colleague from the beginning, agreed to serve as acting president. During his tenure, student self-government expanded its responsibilities. He was supported by Dean of Students Annie E. Hickinbottom, an alumna of the class of 1884. Hickinbottom had chaired the high school French Department and would continue in her position at the college for the next twenty years.

Soon after President Hunter retired, the Board of Education recommended merging Normal College with The City College of New York (CCNY, formerly Free Academy), which had just moved to a new seven-acre campus at Saint Nicolas Heights with space for additional buildings. The once celebrated redbrick building on Sixty-Eighth Street that had housed Normal College was thirty years old. It had been declared a hazard by the fire department and a menace by the health department. These findings were one impetus for the board's recommendation. The board also believed that consolidation of Normal and CCNY would yield economy in the administration of the two colleges. One president, two deans, and one faculty would suffice after the consolidation. A national movement toward coeducation was beginning, but no more than 4 percent of college youth were enrolled in American coeducational institutions. President John Finley of CCNY had no objections to a merger. However, President Gillet and the Associate Alumnae were staunchly opposed.

Their opposition was supported by the Woman Principals' Association, which had many Hunter alumnae members. These women had experienced professional leadership roles that allowed them to think critically about the limited roles prescribed for women in society. They recognized that they had benefited from socializing with women as they pursued their scholarly endeavors at Normal College. They therefore fought to maintain the independence of their alma mater. The Board of Education tabled the plan.

Following his successful opposition to the plan for merger, Gillet focused on improving the college library, which had continued to grow slowly during Thomas Hunter's presidency. In 1898, the calisthenium was converted to a large library, divided into two equal parts: the eastern division housed the alumnae library as well as scientific apparatus donated by the alumnae; the western division housed a library for students. Gillet appointed a committee, chaired by Margaret Barclay Wilson, to review library needs. His appropriation to the library in 1907 was greater than the total expenditure for the preceding five years. Library hours were extended. Instruction was provided in the use of reference books, periodicals were bound, and a bulletin board announcing recent acquisitions was posted. The collection of a few thousand books grew to thirty-one thousand volumes during Wilson's tenure.

Acting President Gillet's contributions to the college were limited as he died suddenly in January 1908. Edward Sanford Burgess, head of the Department of Natural Sciences, succeeded him for a few months. During his time in office, he successfully fought off a second effort by the Board of Education to change the organization of the college. This time, the board sought to separate the NCTD from the college. The plan was rescinded following objections from alumnae and faculty.

On May 4, 1908, George Samler Davis, a graduate of CCNY who had experience as a teacher, principal, and associate superintendent, was installed as the second president of the Normal College. The College had developed significantly since its opening days. It responded to changes in the student body and to developments in the curricula of other colleges. Departmental offerings grew and diversified in the years leading to World War I. Modern languages, always part of the curriculum, remained popular. Classes now included cultural studies as well as reading, writing, and speaking skills. Ancient languages also remained popular. One-third of the student body took one of the eleven courses offered by the popular Classics Department, which now included classical art, architecture, customs, geography, history, and Roman law. All students were required to learn to appreciate music and art. Performance classes in artistic expression were reserved for the talented few. The History Department offered classes in medieval, modern, English, and constitutional history, and the principles of economics. The Math Department, still chaired by Emma Requa, had a double aim: promoting an appreciation of rigorous logic and fostering the understanding of mathematical proof. Science departments attracted women to the study of chemistry, physics, and biology. Field trips were organized for the geology classes. Visits to the American Museum of Natural History were made by several departments.

In recognition of the expanded curriculum, in 1908 the Regents of the State of New York officially acknowledged Normal College as a college of first rank equal to Vassar, Smith, and other women's colleges. In a change of policy, Columbia University announced that it would accept holders of the Normal College BA as candidates for all advanced degrees. Simultaneously, two additional changes took place. In accord with developments in several women's colleges, the organization of student activity was placed under student control, and the faculty was organized into committees and assumed responsibility for many aspects of college administration.

College expenditures increased rapidly from $175,000 in 1900 to $270,000 in 1906, and to $386,820 in 1910. The need for a new building continued to engage the Board of Education, which declared the old building "inadequate and unfit." They adopted a plan to replace the old building, section by section, on its original site. The first step was the demolition of the old NCTD. President Davis supervised the construction of the new NCTD building on Lexington Avenue, between Sixty-Eighth and Sixty-Ninth Streets. He named the building for his predecessor, Thomas Hunter Hall. The planned north building was to have a limestone exterior, a gymnasium with a swimming pool, science laboratories, a library, and a place for outdoor games on the roof. Lack of funding delayed the execution of this plan for decades.

In 1911, a student proctor system was established at Hunter to monitor exams and prevent cheating. The honor system, as it was called, was based on programs established at other colleges. The student leaders included Johanna DeWolf, Edith King, Grace Warren, Helene Esberg, Elizabeth Beutz, and Louise Harvey. Concerned that their work was increasingly seen by students as a "spy system," these students recognized the need to create a constitution for broader self-governance. The resolution proposing the constitution was approved by both college authorities and a large majority of the student body in 1912. "Resolved: that the purpose of the Student Council shall be to form a nucleus of public opinion, and to agitate for the general welfare of the college, in accordance with powers which the Faculty may from time to time grant."

The Student Council approached its responsibilities with energy. It changed the scholarship fund to a loan fund, hoping to assist greater numbers of needy students. It established the Student Council newspaper, the *Bulletin*, to provide regular information to students attending classes at the main building and in the annexes. The council was entrusted with the responsibility of annual publication of the *Wistarion* and the presentation of the Christmas play. The council began to keep a file of students who needed part-time employment to which prospective employers were referred. It developed a proctor system in which ninety students watched over the good conduct of the student body.

As students took on greater responsibilities at Hunter, members of the larger community also became involved in supporting the college. In 1913, in anticipation of the role that the college would later play in the cultural life of New York City, Adolph Lewisohn, the father of a Normal College graduate, donated $10,000 to fund free chamber music concerts under the direction of the Department of Music headed by Professor Fleck, who later gained prominence in the city by virtue of his popular broadcasts of Hunter College recitals on radio station WEAF. The city matched the gift. Concerts opened to the public in the two thousand seat chapel and continued for several seasons.

In recognition of the substantially expanded focus of the college, the board discussed changing its name to New York City College for Women, but the Associate Alumnae protested and demanded that the college be named for its founding president. On April 14, 1914, Normal College was renamed Hunter College. President Hunter died six months later. The new student newspaper, the *Bulletin*, memorialized him: "Here was a man so great . . . that he received recognition even from his contemporaries."

On October 27, 1915, the *Bulletin* addressed the issue of women's suffrage several days before a vote to amend the New York State Constitution to guarantee women the right to vote. An unsigned article, likely written by Adelaide Hahn, who had been elected literary editor of the *Bulletin*, declared women's suffrage to be a matter of "vital importance to all of us." The author recognized that there would be different opinions on the subject and urged all students to study the movement and to take a lively interest in all civic matters. She concluded: "Let us individually do what we can for a higher standard in this great democratic country." Adelaide Hahn was a staunch supporter of suffrage for women, as was her mother, Eleonore Funk Hahn.

There were now six majors available for Hunter students: mathematics, classical languages, French, German, science, and history. English grammar and composition were taught rigorously to all students. The student body, which included more immigrants, relied on Professor Cone for her special class in proper English. Mathematics, chaired by the devoted Professor Requa, was the most popular major. Most Hunter students included a pedagogical component in their studies. The master's (MA) became the minimum requirement for appointment as a tutor to the Hunter College faculty. By 1918, the doctorate (PhD) was required for promotion to the rank of professor.

Mary Meade, a Hunter graduate of 1918, is also exemplary of the students educated in this era. She received an MA in history at Columbia and a PhD in political science at Fordham. She taught history at Curtis High School on Staten Island. In 1937, she was named principal of Tottenville High School, the first woman to head a coeducational high school in New York City. Later she was appointed principal of Washington Irving High School and in 1956 she was appointed assistant superintendent in the high school division of the Board of Education. She served as president of the National Council of Administrative Women in Education from 1956 to 1958. Meade steadily sponsored the advancement of women to administrative posts in the school system.

Meade's reminiscences, written in 1970, provide a thoughtful description of Hunter College during her student years and of the contributions to public education made by her fellow graduates. Meade explained that the professors at Hunter took the pursuit of excellence for granted. In Latin class, professors required accuracy in translations. In English class, professors returned themes with every error underlined. "We had to look up the reason for the error in our textbook, note the rule, rewrite the sentence correctly, and then go on to the important part of the assignment—style, meaning, originality. This was the pattern in all subjects; no slipshod, partially prepared work was accepted in any class. Hunter professors were scholars, and they stretched our minds to a point far ahead of our expectations. They spent time on us, and we knew it."

Meade outlined the rules of her day: Students were permitted to choose a major and a minor course and were required to take courses in other fields. The rules were firm; no one ever thought of questioning them. The textbooks used in classes did not have enough information to complete assignments. Students were expected to use the resources of the city—museums, libraries, public lectures, and historical and artistic centers to supplement their texts.

Meade observed that most students had little money, and the opportunity for a college education was something they aspired to achieve. Thus, college became their life. She noted: "We developed a love for learning, and we pursued it any free time we had left after our regular assignments, home chores, and part-time job were completed. This was a happy life, even in the sad days of WWI." Everyone looked forward to earning a living and to helping younger brothers and sisters advance. Hunter provided an excellent education in the liberal arts and, in addition, opportunities for courses that could be translated into additional resources at a time when the beginning salary for teachers in elementary schools in New York City was $600 a year. Many took the examinations required for prospective teachers at the end of their senior year. The question asked when the scores were posted was not "Did you pass?" but, confident of passing, "How far down on the list are you?"

Meade joined the New York branch of the National Council of Administrative Women in Education and found it to be like a Hunter College alumnae meeting. The New York group was the largest and most active branch of the National Council. Their task was to get more women into managerial positions by encouraging, prodding, and inspiring young women working in city schools. They set up lectures and workshops to help them. Hunter alumnae who had passed the examinations and were running the schools were leaders in inspiring others to become high school principals and assistant superintendents.

Meade observed: "From my 40 years of supervision in NYC schools, I can say that the influence of Hunter-trained teachers can never be overemphasized. They spent out-of-school time in advising their pupils, helping those whose families were in trouble, or running after-school clubs where the religious and intellectual life of boys and girls could be developed and renewed. Many places in the world are the better for the work of Hunter graduates, but the City of New York will find it difficult to assess the debt it owes to the gallant graduates whose college celebrates its centennial in 1970."

Mary Meade died in 1987. Her long life of service is a demonstration of the Hunter culture of excellence and activism. This culture continued to inspire students in the years following American entry into World War I. One thousand Hunter students volunteered to staff the state military census. Their jurisdiction over four assembly districts covered 350,000 inhabitants. Students raised funds to adopt twelve French orphans and made contributions to the British and French War Relief funds. Money was also raised to buy four ambulances; one named for Helen Gray Cone was sent to Italy in the name of the poets of America. In addition to volunteer work, students registered for courses created to meet the war effort: Wireless, Shorthand and Typing, Conversational French, First Aid, Food Dietetics, War Economy, Industrial Chemistry, Bacteriology, and Club Leadership.

Elizabeth Birdie Kallman, a graduate of the class of 1902, centralized college war relief efforts in a joint committee of alumnae, faculty, and students, the Patriotic Service Committee. A dedicated elementary school teacher, and active member of the Alumnae Association, Birdie Kallman chaired the committee. Under her leadership, the committee donated twenty-six hundred books to the New York Public Library, the largest college contribution made, to be distributed to enlisted men and women. A Red Cross auxiliary was established at Hunter with a workroom designated for making surgical dressings, hospital garments, and knitted work. Faculty, students, and alumnae raised over a million and a half dollars in Liberty Loans. The June 1918 Hunter yearbook concluded, "We have started well, but we have not yet really begun to sacrifice. We must work and be ready to give until the war is won for world democracy and permanent peace."

The Department of Art offered a course in mapmaking, given in cooperation with the Geology Department, and produced several graduates for the Army Map Service in Washington, DC. Draftswomen were in high demand by Army recruiters. Several students were selected by Grumman Aircraft for additional specialized training. Others volunteered to make portrait drawings of servicemen. Professor Edna Wells Luetz, Hunter alumna of 1916, taught the new courses in drafting and part of the mapmaking course.

Like many alumnae, Professor Luetz was an immigrant who arrived in New York City at the turn of the century. Born in 1894 in Germany, she was the daughter of an English father and German mother. She attended Normal College High School (later Hunter College High School), graduating in 1912, and received her BA from Hunter College in 1916, winning the annual prize for excellence in German. The following year, she began her professional career at Hunter as a temporary instructor in the Department of Art. She taught a variety of art courses including set design for theatrical productions.

After the war, Professor Luetz obtained both an MA from Columbia and a teacher of fine arts diploma from Teachers College. She continued her studies, learning stage and costume design both in New York City and at the Reinhardt Theatre in Germany. These skills were put to good use in the coming years as she designed production sets in the Hunter College Auditorium and the Hunter College Playhouse (later the Sylvia and Danny Kaye Playhouse). Professor Luetz was elected chairman of the Art Department, serving from 1948 to 1963. She was successful in bringing Robert Motherwell, William Baziotes, Richard Lippold, Ad Reinhardt, Fritz Bultman, George Sugarman, and others to teach at Hunter. Professor Luetz died in 1987.

Emma Requa, Helen Gray Cone, Margaret Barclay Wilson, E. Adelaide Hahn, and Edna Wells Luetz brought the traditions of excellence and activism imbued in their college motto, *Mihi cura futuri*, to successive generations of Hunter students. These students served the war effort through a variety of volunteer and paid activities and later they redoubled their efforts to contribute to a peaceful world. Most Hunter students continued to prepare for teaching careers. Jobs remained available as the population of New York City continued to grow, reaching 5,620,048 residents in 1920. In August of that year, the ratification of the Nineteenth Amendment to the Constitution extended suffrage to all women in the United States. The right to participate fully in American democracy, long advocated by Eleonore Funk Hahn and her daughter E. Adelaide Hahn, was a significant step in the continuing struggle for women's rights. Hunter alumnae were well educated in a variety of fields to fulfill this privilege of citizenship. Committed to excellence and activism, they were prepared to take positions of growing importance in the city, the state, and the nation.

Chapter Two

Excellence and Activism (1920–1929)

In February 1920 Hunter College celebrated its Golden Jubilee. An article in *The New York Herald*, the largest circulation newspaper in the city, reported that in its fifty-year history, Hunter College had graduated twenty-five thousand women, most of whom became teachers in the public schools of the city. Tuition remained free to every New York City girl who completed high school and qualified for admission to the college. The Jubilee ceremonies included the installation of a chapter of the prestigious honor society, Phi Beta Kappa. Hunter was the second women's college, following Vassar, to be recognized with that honor. The college granted its first honorary doctorate that year to beloved alumna, professor, and poet Helen Gray Cone. Finally, a Jubilee exhibit at the New York Public Library brought the storied history of Hunter to all New Yorkers. A brochure printed for the Jubilee listed the nine male members of the Board of Trustees in 1870, and the 1920 Board of Trustees, which in contrast had four female and five male members. The women trustees were all graduates of Hunter College: Mrs. Miriam Sutro Price (class of 1890), Miss Elizabeth S. Williams (class of 1889), Mrs. Mary Gilroy Mulqueen (class of 1884), and Mrs. Ella Wilson Kramer (class of 1876). It included a photo of the Park Avenue building that opened in 1873 and a drawing of a planned new building to meet the growing number of students.

The program for the opening evening included an address by President George S. Davis, music by the Hunter College Orchestra, an address by William Willcox, chairman of the Board of Trustees, and one by Emma D. Huebner, president of the Associate Alumnae. Professor Cone also addressed the audience. The brochure concluded with a list of events for the graduation ceremony held on June 17. Louis Marshall, acclaimed civil rights lawyer and husband of Florence Lowenstein, Hunter alumna class of 1892, addressed the 264 graduates. Among them, twenty-five were recognized for superior academic achievement: twenty-one graduated *cum laude*, three graduated *magna cum laude*, and one graduated *summa cum laude*. Hunter faculty also received recognition that year. Biology professor Margaret Alexander Graham was elected to the New York Academy of Sciences, the first member of the department to receive this honor.

By 1920 Hunter College had grown to thirteen departments and 113 faculty members. Eight of the department chairmen were men and five were women. The women were Christine Reid, art; Helen Gray Cone, English; Emma M. Requa, mathematics; Mabel H. Taylor, physical training; and Margaret B. Wilson, physiology. Most of the faculty were women, with a majority of those having graduated from Hunter College. The tradition of high academic achievement that had been established in the first decades of the college, appreciated so much by Mary Meade, was maintained by the students of the 1920s. Recognition of the students inducted into Phi Beta Kappa and into departmental honorary societies was featured in the *Bulletin*.

The tradition of student self-governance, introduced in 1911, expanded to include a student advisor system to aid freshmen with registration and a charter system to supervise all student clubs. Volunteer war work, which largely precluded other activities from 1917 to 1918, had given student leaders opportunities to engage in civic activism by working with the Patriotic Service Committee. Following the end of the war and the passage of the suffrage amendment, student clubs took on new life.

President Davis supported student clubs and understood that they encouraged initiative, developed responsibility, cultivated judgment, and offered opportunities for the exercise and training of executive ability for those actively engaged. In short, Davis deepened the understanding of the college motto, *Mihi cura futuri*, by emphasizing the importance of action to assure a more just future. Hunter students had always been encouraged to excel in their studies; now they also received support to become campus activists. Among the first student actions was a petition to the faculty to institute a year of compulsory athletics, to add to the physical training course already offered. Many women's colleges had established comprehensive physical education programs in response to, and in reaction against, the widespread belief in women's physical frailties. Hunter student leaders were certainly aware that Barnard College required a physical education class every semester. Comparing physical education at Hunter with that at other women's colleges was an opening to comparisons on issues of student governance, and on political activism beyond the campus.

In November 1921, the Student Council leaders attended an intercollegiate Conference on Disarmament held at Vassar. Sixteen of the twenty-two colleges present were women's colleges: Adelphi, Barnard, Bryn Mawr, Connecticut, Elmira, Goucher, Hunter, Mount Holyoke, New Jersey College for Women, Radcliffe, Russell Sage, Skidmore, Smith, Vassar, Wellesley, and Wheaton. Participation in this conference led Hunter's Student Council to establish a regular college-wide meeting, the Forum, to promote discussion about important issues. The Student Council appointed an Inter-Club Committee, which included representatives from each of the departmental clubs, to invite speakers to address the Forum, which soon held regular presentations featuring faculty members and invited guests. Some of the talks, like that of Professor Sarah Parks of the English Department, were on topics not yet taught in the classroom. Parks's lecture, "The Significance of Race in the World Today," was held on April 21, 1924.

Departmental clubs, many in existence for decades, continued to provide opportunities for friendship and additional learning in the subject of the student's major. The Classical Club, the oldest departmental club, worked to develop faculty-student relationships. Three modern language clubs—French, Italian, and Spanish—put on plays in their respective languages, often inviting alumnae to attend. The German Club raised funds to support Austrian and German students in their war-torn countries. The English Club held weekly meetings for students who wished to improve literary efforts, composition, or dramatics and debating. The composition group worked on a play to submit to an annual contest at the prestigious Century Association. The Music Club invited well-known artists to perform at chapel. The History Club brought speakers on current events.

The Mathematics Club, established by Professor Requa in 1908, continued to stimulate student engagement in mathematical research. It held bimonthly lunch-hour meetings as well as hikes and social events. The Geology Club, organized by Professors Lehnerts and Burgess, invited lectures by noted geologists; it also held monthly social meetings. Meetings of the Kem Club invited well-known chemists to speak. At some meetings, Professor Friedburg presented experiments that were later replicated by students. The club created a chemistry museum that included exhibits presented by industry and produced a journal, *Blast Lamp*, which was recognized by the professional *Chemical Engineering Journal*. The Science Club met twice a month to hear distinguished naturalists and scientists, sometimes on campus and other times at the American Museum of Natural History. Funds raised by the Science Club provided scholarships to send two students to Woods Hole Marine Biological Laboratory on Cape Cod to attend summer courses.

In addition to departmental clubs, two college-wide activities, open to all students, which had their beginnings several years before the Jubilee, continued to develop. Varsity, which became the official name of the college dramatic organization in 1909, was the annual dramatic performance that gradually replaced the Christmas play performed by the senior class until 1914. At first, directed by faculty in the English Department, Varsity performed plays by established playwrights, with cast and crew selected from all interested students. From 1920 until 1929, Henrietta Prentiss, professor of speech and dramatics, and Edna Wells Luetz, professor of art, were the codirectors of Varsity. The most successful play during their years of direction was *The Tempest*, performed in 1927. Faculty and student cooperation was at a high level. The Art Department designed sets and costumes; the Music Department composed original scores; the Speech and Dramatics Department directed the actors. The play was a financial success, earning $3,000 for the Helen Gray Cone Fellowship Fund. In 1921, Make-Up Box was established, an honorary dramatic group of fifty students who were selected by tryouts. Make-Up Box remained the nucleus of all college dramatic activity until 1943.

Similarly, SING was a musical presentation staging competition among the four classes, featuring original lyrics set to contemporary music. The first SING took place in May 1917, with no scenery and no costumes; the audience of faculty and alumnae was enthusiastic. Each year of competition brought new creative effects, attracting larger and larger audiences. Performances were held at large venues including Carnegie Hall, Madison Square Garden, the Roxy Theatre, Radio City Music Hall, and the Metropolitan Opera, until 1941, when annual performances took place at the Assembly Hall in the new building. Performances were enthusiastically reviewed in city newspapers. SING remained an important part of the school year until its final performance in 1959.

In the early 1920s, there were several efforts to create additional opportunities for friendship beyond the athletic meets, the departmental clubs, Varsity, and SING. The establishment of a college orchestra featuring

Figure 2.1. Euripides, *Hippolytus*, 1926. *Source*: Archives and Special Collections, Hunter College Libraries, Hunter College of the City University of New York, New York City.

twelve violinists, one percussionist, one pianist, and a conductor was one such effort. The orchestra performed at chapel, for dance recitals, and for Varsity. Another new college-wide club, the Arts and Crafts Club, supervised by Professor Edna Wells Luetz, worked to improve the artistic quality of all the posters in the college.

The Student Council began to hold open meetings on the first Monday of every month. One outcome of these meetings was a vote to give the Social Services Committee, a group that had developed from a club founded during World War I, permanent representation on the council. Originally established to keep the student body aware of social services work in the city and to cooperate especially with the Lenox Hill Settlement (formerly the Normal College Alumnae House), the Social Services Committee now managed all the philanthropic activities of the council. Membership on this committee consisted of two students from each class, one from each of the religious organizations (the Newman Club, the Young Women's Christian Association, and the Menorah Club) and one from the Pan-Hellenic umbrella, which included sixteen sororities. The Herbert Hoover Relief drive, managed by this committee, raised money to feed hundreds of children each year.

The tradition of daily chapels at Hunter College was replaced by weekly chapels in the 1920s. The Alumnae Association and Student Council were each placed in charge of programming for one chapel meeting. On April 5, 1923, Alumnae Day, hundreds of former students attended chapel. President Davis offered remarks about alumnae professional success. He took pride in the fact that 50 percent of the faculty and staff at Hunter were graduates of the college. The Student Council took on more importance as membership in the Student Union grew. Students wishing to join clubs and sororities were required to join the Student Union. Only union members were entitled to vote for class officers and for Student Council. Members were entitled to free copies of either the *Echo* or the *Bulletin.*

In 1922–1923, the membership of the union reached 94 percent of the student body. The president of the council that year was Mina Rees, class of 1923, who exemplified the twin goals for Hunter College students articulated by President Davis, "excellence and activism." Born in Cleveland, Ohio, in 1902, Mina moved in 1904 to the Bronx with her mother, Alice, an immigrant from England; her father, Moses, a first-generation German American; and four older siblings. Mina excelled as a pupil in elementary school. Her eighth-grade teacher urged her to take the entrance examination for Hunter College High School. She was accepted, and again excelled, graduating as valedictorian in 1919. Mina continued her studies at Hunter College, majoring in mathematics. She answered the queries of some who expressed surprise that she chose that field: "I didn't meet any discouragement at all when I was going into mathematics. Indeed, I didn't know it was a peculiar thing to do. I did what everybody did: pick that field that I found most interesting and decided to major in it."

During her four years as a student at Hunter College, Mina developed strong organizational and social skills that complemented her exceptional intellectual skills. As a sophomore, she played the lead role in a play sponsored by the Pipers, a new alumnae organization eager to bring positive news about Hunter College to the public. The play, *The Duchess of Padua*, by Oscar Wilde, was a great success. In addition to her role as Student Council president, Rees was elected editor of the 1923 *Wistarion*. In her

Figure 2.2. Mina Rees, front right, and sophomore class officers, 1921. *Source*: Archives and Special Collections, Hunter College Libraries, Hunter College of the City University of New York, New York City.

statement as Student Council president in the *Wistarion*, Rees noted, "Participation in student government is the best training for good citizenship."

Believing that every student who participated in student activities found joy in so doing, Rees worked to engage more students in them. The Social Service Associates (previously Social Services Committee) accepted into its ranks all interested students. The Make-Up Box was reorganized to become a dramatics workshop to address all aspects of playwriting, performance, and production, bringing together a large group of students from disparate fields of study. The Inter-Club Committee was given new responsibilities to assist each departmental club organize and find speakers on topics of current importance and interest for the recently established Forum.

As Student Council president, Rees responded to a variety of issues faced by the college. First, she addressed student concerns about the existence of sororities at Hunter. Following three weeks of mass meetings to discuss the matter, a vote was held. Since only 35.5 percent of the students voted to remove the sororities, no change was made in their status. Second, Rees addressed the need to gain greater recognition of the value of Hunter College to the citizens of New York. She announced a gift of $500 from the Student Council to the college to be used to secure a press agent. The concern for college publicity was taken up by future leaders of the Student Council through the creation of the Journalism Club.

Rees also led student efforts to speak out on national issues. In March 1923, the Student Council sent a proposal to Congress urging the federal government to limit or prohibit the labor of children:

> Whereas, according to the census of 1920, there are over one million child laborers between the ages of ten and fifteen in the United States;
>
> Whereas these children are being exploited far beyond their years;
>
> Whereas, in addition, hundreds of children under ten years of age are laboring in cotton, sugar beet and onion fields, in street trades and tenement sweatshops;
>
> . . .
>
> Whereas child labor is unjust, unnecessary, and a waste of the nation's future citizenship;
>
> . . .
>
> Therefore, be it resolved that the Student Self-Government Association of Hunter College of the City of New York urge the amendment of our Federal Constitution in order that the Congress shall have power, concurrent with several states, to limit or prohibit the labor of children.

Hunter students were aware of immigrant children working in New York City. They read about children working on farms in other parts of the country. As the recipients of free schooling, including free college education, they actively supported all children who were deprived of an education.

While still a freshman Rees was asked to teach a trigonometry lab course in surveying. To do a good job, she registered for summer classes at Teachers College. She taught for the next three years at half the pay of the beginning instructor's salary. Despite her teaching duties and her heavy student activities calendar, Rees maintained very high grades and was elected a member of Phi Beta Kappa. For her multiple achievements, teaching, student leadership, and academic excellence, she was awarded the prestigious H Pin for her contribution to Hunter College as president of the Student Council and graduated *summa cum laude*.

Following graduation, Rees was placed on the list of twenty-six candidates eligible for jobs to teach high school mathematics. Fifteen of the graduates on the list, including Sara Malkin, who placed first, were Hunter alumnae. Rees was also offered a full-time job teaching mathematics at Hunter College. She declined, saying that she didn't know enough to teach at the college level. She accepted a job at Hunter College High School, simultaneously taking graduate classes in math at Columbia. She decided to pursue a PhD at Columbia, taking four of the six-credit required classes, before she learned that Columbia was not interested in having women candidates for the PhD in mathematics. This was a traumatic experience for Rees who had not experienced discrimination until that moment. Her response was practical. She revised her program and received an MA in education in 1925 from Teachers College.

Rees started teaching at Hunter College at that point and by 1929 had saved enough money to begin a full-time PhD program in algebra. She took a leave of absence from Hunter and enrolled at the University of Chicago, completing her PhD in December 1931, and returning to New York to become an instructor at Hunter College. She was promoted to assistant professor in 1932 and to associate professor in 1940. She taught diverse undergraduate courses including geometry, calculus, and experimental mathematics.

Rees did not publish any mathematical research from 1932 to 1942, but she did contribute reviews to *Scripta Mathematica*, whose editor, Lao G. Simons, was also on the Hunter math faculty. She contributed reviews to the American Mathematical Society and the Mathematics Association of America. Rees recognized that her forte was in teaching and administration, rather than research. She attended the meetings of several mathematics groups and made many friendships. She met Leopold Brahdy, a physician, in 1936. They married in 1955.

In 1943, the Applied Mathematics Panel, created by the US Office of Scientific Research and Development to support war-related research, needed a skilled mathematician and administrator. Richard Currant, a mathematician and friend, recommended Rees to Applied Mathematics Panel director Warren Weaver as someone who could fill both needs. Rees was offered the job and took a second leave of absence from Hunter to become technical aide and executive assistant to Weaver. The Applied Mathematics Panel team met in the Empire State Building, writing and overseeing contracts between the government and research universities. Their most significant initiative was early developmental work on computers and computing. The Applied Mathematics Panel was disbanded in 1946 and its role in supporting scientific research was transferred to the new Office of Naval Research. Rees was appointed to head its Mathematics Branch and moved to Washington, DC. She was the first woman in the new field of grant administration. In 1948, Rees and Weaver were each awarded the King's Medal of Britain for service in the cause of freedom, and the Presidential Certificate by President Truman. The following year, the Mathematics Branch expanded into the Mathematical Sciences Division, with Rees still at the helm. By 1952 she was appointed deputy science director of the Office of Naval Research. Through her position she made policy and funding decisions in the development of rocket propulsion and the design and engineering of hydrofoil craft and high-speed computers.

In 1953, Rees returned to Hunter College as professor of mathematics and dean of faculty. In 1961, she was named dean of graduate studies at CUNY (City University of New York). In 1968 she became provost of the new Graduate Division of CUNY. The following year she became the first president of the Graduate School and University Center of CUNY. When Rees began her presidency, the graduate program at CUNY had only four majors: chemistry, economics, English, and psychology. By 1971, when she retired, it had twenty-six doctoral programs. Rees was particularly devoted to women graduate students, perhaps reflecting her experience of discrimination when she was a PhD student at Columbia. She promoted part-time employment and study for women with children as well as day care centers. Throughout her life, Rees was a model for the twin qualities she had learned as a student at Hunter College: excellence and activism.

Rees continued her involvement with many committees to improve science and science education in the US. In 1971 she was elected president of the American Association for the Advancement of Science, the first woman so honored. She created research assistantships for graduate students, research associateships for post-docs, secretarial assistance, travel support, summer salaries, sabbatical leaves, release time, and funding for two journals, *Mathematical Reviews* and *Applied Mathematical Reviews.* Mina Rees died in 1997. The library at the CUNY Graduate Center bears her name.

Two years after Rees completed her term as Student Council president, Bella Visono (Dodd) was elected president of the Student Union. During her term, 1924–1925, the proctor system adopted by the student body in 1923 was renamed the honor system. Each new student was required to sign the Honor Code, which stated: "We, the students of Hunter College, will strive to uphold individually and collectively the honor of this college in our academic work. We will do all in our power to maintain a high standard of honor in our secondary activities and direct our best effort toward creating a spirit of honesty and honor for its own sake." Hunter students presented a paper on the honor system at a meeting of the Women's Intercollegiate Self-Government Association held at Oberlin in 1924. Hunter was selected to represent the Association at the Young Women's Christian Association (YWCA) conference in New York City in April.

Bella Visono was born in 1904 in Picerno, a village in southern Italy. She was brought up by a wet nurse, who became her foster mother, and a shepherd, who became her foster father. When Bella was six, her mother came from New York to take her to the Bronx to join her family of Italian immigrants. She learned to speak English from an older sister and enrolled in elementary school. In the fall of 1916, as she was preparing to attend Evander Childs High School, Bella had a bad accident getting off a trolley that led to amputation of her left foot and a year's convalescence. She began high school using crutches and ultimately was able to walk with a poorly designed prosthesis. Despite her physical problems, she received good grades in history and science and was voted the most popular girl in her class. The latter meant a lot to her. She also won a state scholarship that helped with living expenses when she attended Hunter College.

Bella took the Pelham Bay subway line, newly extended to her Bronx neighborhood, to the college each day. She decided to become a teacher. In her memoir, written thirty years after her freshman year, she described her first college wardrobe: two dresses, a blue voile and a gingham; a black skirt; two sweaters knitted by her mother; and a large collection of starched white collars that she wore with the sweaters. She was not conscious of having an inadequate wardrobe. The students at Hunter, even those from better-off families, she thought, were more interested in things of the mind than in fancy clothing.

The teacher who made the greatest impact on Bella's life was Sarah Parks who taught her two semesters of freshman English. Parks was different from the rest of the well-mannered faculty. She arrived at Hunter without a hat, her straight blond hair flying in the wind as she rode along Park Avenue on her bicycle. Dean Annie Hickinbottom, who lectured the students on the importance of wearing hats and gloves, would have been scandalized if a student had imitated Miss Parks. Had she known the content of Parks's classes, she would have been deeply concerned by her social theories. Miss Parks spoke about the Russian Revolution, comparing it to the French Revolution, which she believed had opened European culture to vast changes. Similarly, she thought that the Russian Revolution would lead to improved living standards for all people. She brought books on communism to class and loaned them to students who wished to read them.

In her memoir, Bella noted that her thinking began to change during her first year at Hunter. She studied science and the evolution of man and society. She developed a strong sense of responsibility for social reform and became skeptical of religious concepts. She and her friends regarded themselves as the avant-garde of a new culture. Her best friend was Ruth Goldstein (Weintraub). They met in the basement of the Park Avenue building, a room that students transformed into an informal tearoom and meeting place. They discussed revolution, sex, philosophy, and religion. They hoped to build "a new world" to replace the current "selfish" one. Outside the halls of Hunter on the streets of New York, the Roaring Twenties, with girls dressed in flapper costumes and short haircuts, were increasingly visible. Inside the halls, sedate young women still strolled companionably and quietly. But in the basement of Hunter there was talk of revolution.

During the summer after her freshman year, Bella found a job to help pay for her expenses. She was hired to sell the *Volume Library*, a children's encyclopedia. She rented a room in a farmer's home in Mount Kisco to be able to reach potential customers in Westchester. When she returned to Hunter, her ideas had matured. She had lived on her own and earned her way. She spoke of science and evolution; she was skeptical of religious ideas. She thought those who believed in a Creator were anti-intellectual. Though she no longer had Sarah Parks as a teacher, she continued to speak with her and to seek her advice.

Bella and several of her friends became involved with student government. She attended an intercollegiate conference at Vassar College with Mina Rees, as representatives of the Student Council, where the main topics of discussion were sororities and whether they should be abolished, and the possibility of establishing an honor system. Bella was elected president of Student Council, 1924 to 1925, her senior year. She led the movement to establish the honor system. She also brought national politics into student self-government by conducting a straw poll for the presidential elections of 1924. Robert M. La Follette, the Progressive candidate, won the election at Hunter. Professor Hannah Egan of the Education Department was one faculty member who thought that change was happening too fast in the college. She challenged Bella about her lack of attendance in the Catholic girls' organization, the Newman Club. Bella explained that she was modern; she followed scientific ideas. She assured Professor Egan that she planned to spend her life serving mankind.

During Bella Visono's term of office new clubs were created by the Student Council including the Hunter chapter of the League of Nations Association, New Discussion Club, Debating Club, and Play Shop. In addition, the Press Board, a committee of nine students, each assigned as correspondents to a daily newspaper, was created to report all the news about Hunter College that would be of interest to New Yorkers. Photographers from the AP began to appear on campus to record athletic events and other activities. The Pre-Medical Association was opened with a large membership offering lectures and social events. The Student Exchange, which had operated for six years as a purveyor of fudge and cookies, was expanded to allow sale of those and other items, including gym clothes. A manager was hired to supervise the operation, which provided revenue for the Student Council. Traditional events from prior years continued: the

Figure 2.3. Bella Visono Dodd, front row, fifth from left, and the Student Council, 1925. *Source*: Archives and Special Collections, Hunter College Libraries, Hunter College of the City University of New York, New York City.

college boat ride, senior-faculty teas, Ice Carnival, Junior Council parties, Alumnae Day, Varsity, and SING.

Bella Visono and Ruth Goldstein (Weintraub) graduated with honors in 1925. They enrolled in summer session at Columbia University, beginning work on their MA degrees. That autumn, Bella's first teaching job was as a substitute teacher in the History Department of Seward Park High School on the Lower East Side. She taught six classes of medieval and European history. The students were unruly at first, throwing chalk and erasers, but she worked hard to stimulate interest, and she was able to win their cooperation. She asked her pupils to bring newspapers to class and started lively discussions of current events. At the end of the semester, Bella received a note from Professor Edgar Dawson, chairman of the History Department at Hunter, offering her an instructorship. Bella Visono and Ruth Goldstein (Weintraub), who received a similar offer, returned to teach at Hunter in February 1926. They also continued their studies at Columbia, doing graduate work in political science and taking new courses focused on the role of the press in creating public opinion. They brought ideas from their graduate classes to their Hunter classrooms and soon began to send students out in pairs to visit courtrooms and jails. Bella remained influenced by the poverty of the high school pupils she had taught. She began to believe that radical change was necessary.

Bella began to frequent International House, a popular gathering spot for foreign students near Columbia, and felt a desire to be a citizen of the world. She moved closer to communist ideology with its emphasis on internationalism. She also spent many hours at both the Columbia library and the New York Public Library working on her master's thesis, which sought to answer this question: "Is Congress a Mirror of the Nation?" She read hundreds of brief biographies in the *Congressional Directory* and found that many congressmen had started as poor boys, had struggled to obtain an education, and had spent some time teaching. Yet they had done nothing, she thought, to change the conditions of the poor they represented.

In the summer of 1927, after receiving MA degrees, Bella and Ruth rented a cottage in the Adirondacks. Friends came to spend long weekends of conversation and swimming in Lake Schroon. It was a time of deep thinking for the young women. Bella and Ruth returned to New York City in the fall. Disappointed by the lack of change in the lives of impoverished Americans, they decided to become lawyers to be able to represent those who remained unrepresented. The two Hunter friends registered at NYU School of Law. During their three years of law school, Bella and Ruth continued to teach at Hunter College. Bella enjoyed being not only an instructor but an adviser to many of her students.

Having passed the bar exam, Bella took a leave of absence from her job at Hunter in 1930 to serve a clerkship to qualify for admission to the New York Bar. In September, she married John Dodd whom she had met while traveling in Europe the previous summer. John was ten years older than Bella. He had served in the Air Force during World War I. By 1932, she returned to teaching at Hunter and soon became involved in organizing the Hunter College Instructors Association. She was elected its representative to the Faculty Council.

The following year, 1933, the United States recognized the Soviet Union. Communist students around the nation became active on college campuses, including Hunter, demanding the right to meet. Bella remained a leader of the Hunter College Instructors Association and was increasingly attracted by the selfless devotion of members of the Communist Party. Ruth, Bella's close friend of many years, warned her about the undemocratic nature of the communists, critical of their belief in a one-party system. Bella replied that she was convinced that the communists were the only ones fighting to improve the "rotten conditions" of today. Ruth Goldstein Weintraub was no less eager to improve the lives of impoverished communities but took a different route. She remained on the faculty at Hunter and simultaneously worked on her doctoral degree at NYU, which she received in 1939. She was promoted to professor, went on to become chairman of the Department of Political Science, and the founding dean of the Division of Social Sciences. She established the Department of Urban Studies in the division and as well as an interdisciplinary program in Jewish Social Studies.

Bella became an official of the New York City Teachers Union. In spring 1936 she took a six-month leave of absence from her teaching position at Hunter to serve as the legislative representative of the union, spending most of her time in Albany, in Washington, DC, and at City Hall in New York. She met regularly with leaders of the Communist Party and of the American Federation of Labor. In the May Day parade of 1936 more than five hundred teachers marched with the communists. Bella was one of them. In 1938, her work for the union was so demanding that she decided to resign from Hunter to take a full-time job with the union. President Colligan urged her to reconsider her decision. She replied forthrightly: “In this country one hundred and forty million Americans have no tenure and no security. I’ll take my chances with them.”

For the next eight years Bella worked for the union at the modest weekly wage of $60. Her marriage unraveled in 1940, but Bella was so consumed by her work that she took little time to grieve. On October 24 she spoke at a peace rally at Hunter College. The rally was planned by a group of fifteen student leaders including the Student Council president, Bella Savitsky (Abzug). She continued to work with the American Labor Party and with the Communist Party leadership. By the end of World War II, Bella Dodd no longer believed that the solution to the horrors of poverty was to be found in communism. She hoped to drift away quietly from the Communist Party. Instead, in June 1949, she was publicly denounced and expelled. In the next few years, she tried to make sense of her life. She read and slowly built a law practice defending workers. She reconciled with the Catholic Church of her childhood. Before she died in 1969, Bella Visono Dodd wrote a memoir explaining her complicated decisions.

One year after Bella’s graduation, Hunter’s annual budget reached $1 million. President Davis appointed two new deans, Professor Lewis D. Hill, academic dean, and Professor James M. Kieran, dean of education, to meet the needs of the growing numbers of students. Another administrative change took place that year. The College would no longer report to the Board of Education, because a Board of Higher Education had been established to “furnish the benefits of collegiate education gratuitously to citizens” who were residents of New York. The board was to have twenty-one members selected by the mayor for nine-year terms. The board had the right to accept gifts from private sources for the welfare of the colleges under its control; at that time there were only two, Hunter College and The City College of New York (former Free Academy).

Throughout the 1920s the Park Avenue building continued to deteriorate as evening, extension, and summer sessions served thousands of students who needed classrooms and study space. Only one of the planned three replacement sections had been completed before US entry into World War I, Thomas Hunter Hall, facing Lexington Avenue. Although President Davis made use of annexes in Brooklyn, Queens, and Staten Island, overcrowding forced him to limit entry to the college. In January 1925, the Associate Alumnae sought the support of the New York Federation of Women’s Clubs in a fund-raising campaign. Davis issued a roster of Hunter alumnae who had made substantial contributions to New York City and more broadly, among them Helen A. Messenger, physicist; Marie K. Gallagher, educator; E. Adelaide Hahn, classicist; Marjorie M. Almond, professor of medicine; Ruth Lewinson, distinguished lawyer; Yan MacLeod, sculptor and second woman medalist at the Salon des Artistes Français; Gertrude Purcell, actress-playwright; Agnes M. Craig, first woman justice of the New York Municipal Court and a member of the Teachers' Retirement Board; and Rosalie Loew Whitney, justice of the Court of Domestic Relations. Davis reasoned that the alma mater of these distinguished citizens should remain on Park Avenue.

As no final decision had been made, the campaign to keep Hunter College in Manhattan continued. On January 5, 1927, the front page of the *Bulletin* carried a bold headline: "Hunter World's Largest Woman's College Urgently Needs New Building, 12,146 Girls Campaign." A drawing of the planned building on Park Avenue included a twenty-two-story tower. The first-page article explained that the present situation, which included multiple annexes in Manhattan, Brooklyn, and Queens, was economically wasteful. By using the entire Park Avenue campus, students reported that the new building could serve eight thousand students. A chart illustrated that 38 percent of the students lived in Manhattan, 29 percent in the Bronx, 24 percent in Brooklyn, 6 percent in Queens, and 2 percent in Staten Island. A graph predicted that in 1930 there would be six thousand students attending the day session at Hunter.

In response to continued pressure the Board of Higher Education authorized an architect to draw up new plans for the Park Avenue campus. Estimates for the cost of construction reached $2.25 million, leading some members of the board to return to the plan to sell the Park Avenue site. Land near the Jerome Reservoir in the Bronx had been set aside for the college. It would be much less expensive to build there. President Davis, faculty, students, and the alumnae were strongly in favor of remaining at Sixty-Eighth Street. Despite continuing opposition to relocation, an allocation of $1.5 million was made to the project of constructing new college buildings in the Bronx. A second allocation of an equal amount was soon added.

The *Bulletin* continued to devote articles to the need for additional academic space for Hunter students; it also reported regularly on club activities, athletic events, debates sponsored by the Ottinger Debating Society, and on prizes and awards won by students and alumnae. In April 1926, the *Bulletin* informed students that the English Department would offer a journalism class the following semester. Recognizing journalism as a potential source of employment for Hunter graduates, the newspaper featured several articles about the topic. Professor Blanche Colton Williams gave a talk to the Journalism Club about magazine writing, which was featured on May 26, 1927. She advised, "The most powerful weapon in any author's struggle for recognition is thorough knowledge of some subject. . . . Choose your field and specialize." Agnes Dunn, a reporter on *The Standard Union*, offered advice based on her newspaper experience. "When the *Standard Union* offered me a position as Society Editor, I seized the opportunity regardless of the fact that I knew nothing about society editing. . . . Two weeks later I became Assistant Editor on the Women's Page." For a while she served as dramatics editor, covering amateur companies in Brooklyn and New York. She was advised to refrain from negative comments as her review also served advertising purposes. Dunn recommended the journalism class she had taken at Hunter.

Students advocated a major in journalism. They presented their ideas in an editorial in the June 1928 *Echo*. Not daunted by the limited number of positions open to women on newspapers, the editorial recommended providing journalism students with a very strong program. To guarantee strong writing skills, journalism majors would be selected by English Department faculty. Prerequisites would include stenography and typing, which students might master outside of college or in extension courses. By covering regular assignments for the *Bulletin*, by working as correspondents for the city newspapers, in conjunction with the Journalism Club, and by doing freelance work of all kinds, students would gain practical training to supplement the thorough theoretical knowledge of the lecture hall. Francis S. Hershfeld, editor-in-chief of the *Echo*, concluded: "If nearly all roads at Hunter lead to Pedagogy, cannot one, at least, lead to Plumedom?"

Students who followed the advice of Professor Williams and Ms. Dunn and built careers in journalism included S. F. Porter in financial journalism and Ada Louise Huxtable in architectural journalism, both of whom are profiled in later chapters. Others who similarly created new niches in journalism included Rose Nadler Franzblau, Lenore Oppenheimer Hershey, Judith Klein Crist, and Ruby A. Saunders.

Rose Nadler Franzblau, class of 1926, who majored in psychology, completed both an MA and a PhD in psychology at Columbia University. Franzblau dispensed advice on emotional life in newspapers, on radio and TV, and in popular magazines. In 1951, Dorothy Schiff, New York's first female publisher, who had also attended a women's college, Bryn

Mawr, recruited her to create an advice column in the *New York Post*. Her popular column ran for twenty-five years and was syndicated in a dozen newspapers across the country.

Students in the ensuing decades followed journalism experience at Hunter into lifetime careers in the field. Lenore Oppenheimer Hershey, class of 1937, majored in journalism. She was assigned by Professor Emma K. Temple as college correspondent to *The New York Times*. Following graduation, she began her career in the promotion department of the *Herald Tribune*. She moved to *McCall's* magazine in 1952 and left as executive editor in 1968, later moving to the *Ladies' Home Journal* as managing editor. In 1973, she was appointed editor-in-chief, three years after feminists had staged a daylong sit-in demanding that a woman be given that position. Her seminars on the role of women in the economy led President Nixon to establish in 1972 a Presidential Advisory Committee on the Economic Role of Women, on which she served.

Judith Klein Crist, class of 1941, majored in English and was a prolific contributor to the *Echo*. Following graduation, she was an English instructor at Washington State University and an English instructor for the Air Force. She returned to New York, enrolled at the Columbia School of Journalism, and received an MA in 1945. Her first job as a journalist was as assistant to the women's editor at the *Herald Tribune*. In 1957 she began to contribute theater reviews. During the 1963 newspaper strike she reviewed theater and movies for WABC. When the strike ended, the *Tribune* hired her as movie critic. She later was the founding film critic for *New York Magazine* and then joined *TV Guide* for twenty-two years, where her reviews reached a readership of more than twenty million people. She was the *Today* show's first regular movie critic, becoming a fixture on NBC from 1963 to 1973.

Ruby A. Saunders, class of 1950, majored in journalism. Her first job following graduation was as editorial assistant at *Parents' Magazine* Enterprises. She later became managing editor of *Calling All Girls*, remaining there from 1963 to 1979, by which time it had changed its name to *Young Miss*. Saunders wrote many books for young adults including a series about Marilyn Morgan, RN. They were published by New American Library's Signet Nurse Romances. These books were the first nurse stories about a Black nurse written by a Black author.

The *Bulletin*, the *Echo*, and the *Wistarion* provided opportunities for student authors to publish their writings. Some of these authors reported on the concerns of immigrant families that could be met by Hunter students.

On March 10, 1927, the *Bulletin* called attention to "Bully's Neediest Cases." A writer reported that the Student Council had received a call from the Bureau of Children's Charities requesting two volunteers. The first would work with an eight-year-old Jewish boy whose mother worked all day and therefore had no time for him. He lived on Third Street and Avenue D. The boy had fallen behind in reading at school. The second would work with an eleven-year-old boy, a member of a struggling Spanish family, who had difficulty with English. He lived on 174th Street in the Bronx. Students who wished to volunteer to work with these boys were encouraged to leave a note in the Social Service Box in the Council Room.

Hunter students in the 1920s were also entertained and informed by stories in the *Echo*. Students interested in writing submitted pieces for review by student editors. Libbie Israelite, who graduated in 1924, began to submit stories to the *Echo* during her first year at Hunter and continued to publish stories regularly, joining the *Echo* literary staff in November 1922 and ultimately being elected by her peers as editor-in-chief in October 1923. She held her position until January 1924. Among the many stories she submitted was a piece published in May 1924, just before her graduation, "The Young Woman of Great Expectations." The story, written in the first person, posed the dilemma of a girl who expected fame as a creative writer, but settled for life as a teacher and wife.

In a story sure to resonate with many of Libbie's classmates, the author reviewed the unrealistic expectations of success as a writer harbored by her immigrant family. She was the "bright little girl who always got AAA." Having won a contest for a poem about milk, sponsored by the Borden Company, the young author was pressed by her parents to perform. She became the storyteller on her block. But her later efforts to write did not receive approval from friends or publishers. In the story, the protagonist became a high school French teacher. Unable to write, she turned to another creative outlet, painting. At an exhibition she met a famous young novelist from Indiana and was happily married. This story by the prolific student author and editor of the *Echo* was a warning to student journalists that not all would succeed in their hopes of becoming professionals of "Plumedom."

George Samler Davis served for two decades as president of Hunter College. During his tenure Hunter College was accredited by the Association of American Universities, the Association of Colleges and Secondary Schools of the Middle States and Maryland, and the American Council on Education. Alumnae were now automatically eligible for membership in the American Association of University Women. Professor Helen Gray Cone, chair of the English Department from 1899 to 1927, captured the essence of the changes in the spirit of Hunter College brought about by President Davis:

> Hunter College escaped from her isolation. . . . In the olden days we were figuratively speaking, surrounded by high walls. The walls were not prison walls but crowned with hedges, and we could see the sky. But the walls shut us in. Then, wanting a larger vision, some of us formed a stairway, and climbing up, envisaged a larger view, a view of students and of colleges the world over. We realized then that the walls must be broken down, that the College must take its place in a changing world.

Two of the graduates of 1928, in different ways, exhibited the spirit suggested by Professor Cone, Edna Patricia Flannery (Kelly) and Marion Wilson (Starling). Flannery was born in 1906 in East Hampton, the youngest of five daughters raised by Irish immigrant parents, Patrick Joseph Flannery, a horticulturist, and Mary Ellen McCarthy Flannery. Edna graduated from East Hampton High School in 1924 and attended Hunter College from 1924 to 1928, receiving a BA in history and economics. In the fall of 1928 she married Edward Leo Kelly, a Brooklyn lawyer. The couple raised two children, William and Maura. In January 1942, New York governor Herbert Lehman appointed Edward Kelly as a judge on the New York City court. Less than eight months later, Kelly was killed in an automobile crash.

After his death, Edna considered a career in politics. She had a powerful ally in Irwin Steingut, then the minority leader in the New York Assembly and Brooklyn's political boss. Steingut encouraged the thirty-six-year-old widow to become active in local political organizations. She reorganized the women's auxiliary of the ailing Madison Democratic Club and served as research director for the New York State legislature from 1943 to 1949. In 1944 Edna Kelly was elected to the first of three terms on the Democratic executive committee of Kings County, New York, and joined Steingut as a coleader of the 18th Assembly District.

On July 15, 1949, Kings County Democratic leaders chose Kelly as their nominee to fill the vacancy caused by the death of Brooklyn-based US Representative Andrew L. Somers. Local leaders were eager to put a woman on the ballot to recognize the work of women for the party. The district contained large Catholic and Jewish populations and was heavily Democratic. Kelly supported President Truman's domestic and foreign policies, pledging to back US participation in the United Nations as well as continued financing for the Marshall Plan, aid to Israel, and entry into NATO. On the domestic side, Kelly focused on issues of interest to women, advocating federal dollars for the development of childcare centers and an investigation into high milk prices; she opposed excise taxes on cosmetics.

Kelly was elected in November 1949, becoming the first Hunter alumna to serve in the US Congress. She was also the first Democratic woman to represent Brooklyn. She stressed her credentials as a representative of all district constituents, not just women. She implored, "Please don't describe me as attractive. . . . Just say I have common sense!"

In Washington, Kelly asked for and won an assignment on the Foreign Affairs Committee, where she served for twenty years, supporting a broad array of American Cold War policies ranging from the creation of NATO to intervention in the Vietnamese civil war. Her first vote in Congress in early 1950 was in favor of a bill to increase aid to South Korea; it failed. Kelly continued to establish herself as an implacable foe of communism. In summer 1955 she visited the Geneva Summit, the first Soviet-US-Atlantic summit of the Cold War. On the home front, she supported the House Committee on Un-American Activities, arguing that it "performed good service." In her 1954 campaign, Kelly defeated Republican Abraham Sher, winning 76.8 percent of the vote.

Kelly became chair of the Foreign Affairs Subcommittee on Europe in 1955 and led the first of five fact-finding missions to Europe and the Middle East. She introduced legislation denouncing religious persecution in Eastern Europe. She urged the US to play a more aggressive role in mediating Arab-Israel peace accords through the UN. As chair of the Subcommittee on Europe, Congresswoman Kelly supported a hardline approach to America's rivals in the Kremlin and to Soviet-sponsored regimes throughout the world. She eventually chaired a subcommittee on the Canada-US Interparliamentary Group and was secretary of the House Democratic Caucus. In 1967 she was appointed to the newly formed Committee on Standards of Official Conduct and helped draft its standards.

In 1963, President Kennedy appointed her a member of the US delegation to the UN where she worked closely with UN Ambassador Adlai Stevenson. At the time of her retirement, she was the third-ranked member of the Foreign Affairs Committee. In the mid-sixties, shifting demographics and the decline of the once-powerful New York City Democratic machine threatened Kelly's safe seat. She narrowly survived a primary challenge from a Flatbush politician who attacked her pro–Vietnam War votes and what he described as her anti-Israel position. In the general election she won again with 73 percent of the vote.

In 1968, the New York legislature divided her district into two: Shirley Chisholm ran in one and Emanuel Celler in the other. Kelly decided not to run against Chisholm. Rather than retire, she mounted a primary challenge against Emanuel Celler, a forty-five-year veteran in the House. She lost and claimed that Celler supporters tried to intimidate her with a dirty campaign. Kelly returned to her home in the Crown Heights section of Brooklyn and helped coordinate a Library of Congress oral history project with former US representatives. She resided in Brooklyn until 1981 when illness forced her to move to Alexandria, Virginia, to live with her daughter. Kelly died in 1997.

Marion Elizabeth Wilson (Starling), Kelly's classmate, was born in 1907 in Zion, Illinois, a Catholic evangelical community of twenty thousand just north of Chicago. Her father, an acclaimed organist, had been hired to play at the Tabernacle, a church built to accommodate eight-thousand parishioners. The Wilson family was the only Black family in the city. Marion Wilson recalled no racial discrimination, but rather a feeling of being special because of her father's position. At an early age she became aware of her family's feeling that Blackness was to be discounted. If one was to amount to something, it was better to have white friends. Social status was dependent on minimizing one's racial identity. Marion commented on the embarrassment experienced by her parents when Mr. Wilson's father arrived for a visit. Trying to impress their neighbors with the status of the Wilson family, Marion's parents had told everyone that Grandpa Wilson was a civil engineer. Grandpa, who had been freed from slavery at the age of ten, proudly announced that he was a janitor at P.S. 9 in Brooklyn.

Marion was the eldest of six children. She was the only one who remembered hearing her grandfather talk about a childhood event in his small dining room in Brooklyn. Grandpa Wilson spoke of the day when "Master" had brought all the slaves together in the "Big House" and told them that they were free. In the pandemonium that ensued, the boy was pushed aside, not understanding what was going on. When the slave owner came at him, shouting "You are FREE!," he crashed into a large hall mirror.

When Marion was sixteen, the family moved back to Brooklyn. Though she had been a stellar high school student, college seemed to be out of reach as Marion was expected to work to help support the family.

Learning that Hunter College was tuition-free, her plan changed. She registered for classes and worked part time. Marion was now expected to get a teaching license so that she would have a secure income to help the family. She was an excellent student at Hunter College, majoring in Greek and Latin, graduating Phi Beta Kappa, the first Black student to receive this honor. Marion also participated in clubs. She was a member of the Classical Club and vice-president of the Journalism Club. She joined the Make-Up Box. The professor who had the greatest influence on her, Professor Adele Bildersee, Hunter alumna class of 1903, taught in the English Department.

Bildersee saw in Marion a student of exceptional ability who was pretending to believe what she thought was expected of her, not what she truly felt as a Black woman. She challenged Marion to examine critically

Figure 2.4. Marion Wilson Starling, 1928. *Source*: Archives and Special Collections, Hunter College Libraries, Hunter College of the City University of New York, New York City.

the path chosen for her by her family. Marion's classes with Bildersee marked a critical turning point in her life. She remembered, "Had I not had this perceptive, caring, and tough woman for a teacher, nothing would have happened to me. I would have gone on to be a shallow person doing what my mother told me to do." Immediately following graduation in June 1928, Marion enrolled at Columbia with the objective of obtaining an MA in English. Mrs. Wilson was pleased. With an MA in English, her daughter would be put on the list of eligible candidates for a high school English job.

Marion received her MA in 1929 and consulted Adele Bildersee and W. E. B. DuBois, a Harvard-educated PhD in sociology and a family friend, about a job offer to teach English at Spelman College in Atlanta. Both urged her to take the job, telling her that she needed to learn about her roots. Her mother was furious, but Marion left Brooklyn for Atlanta. She taught at Spelman from 1930 to 1943 and believed that she learned more from her students than she taught them. At Spelman, she taught English and speech. She also taught at nearby Morris Brown College, offering classes in African American literature and history. Marion married Earl Alvin Starling, a colleague in the Music Department at Morris Brown, in 1934. A daughter, Tiffany, was born to this short-lived union.

Taking a leave of absence from Spelman, Marion returned to New York City and registered in the doctoral program in English at NYU. She thought about writing a dissertation about slave narratives. Many in the world of academe shared her mother's view that the topic wasn't worthy of exploration. Starling, however, was influenced by her education at Hunter and at Spelman and by the stories of torture and killing in occupied Europe reported in the morning newspapers of 1943, which reminded her of the horror recorded in slave narratives. She ultimately submitted her dissertation with the title "The Slave Narrative: Its Place in American Literary History." In 1943, when she began to do her research, she knew of only one slave narrative, that of Frederick Douglass. One of her professors asked her, "How many slave narratives are there?" She decided to find out. She was unaware that there were no narratives lined up in libraries awaiting her perusal.

Her research was aided by the Folklore Division of the Federal Writers' Project, established to create jobs during the Depression. From 1933 to 1938 oral interviews with twenty-five hundred former slaves were collected by the Folklore Division in seventeen states. Ten thousand pages of documents stored in barrels in the basement of the Library of

Congress, the Slave Narrative Collection, remained off limits to scholars until 1944. Historians continued to doubt the authenticity of slave narratives, convinced that most had been sensationalized by abolitionists to bolster support for their cause. Once the Slave Narrative Collection was open to scholars, opinions began to change. Decades later, two of the most respected Black historians, John W. Blassingame and Charles T. Davis, concluded that Starling's impeccably researched 1946 dissertation inaugurated the modern era of African American historical writing with its focus on giving voice to the oppressed.

Her achievement had several levels. First, she discovered thousands of previously unknown narratives. Second, she classified the narratives, separating those printed before 1836 from those that were likely influenced by abolitionists. The earlier narratives described the adventures of individuals, and the later ones added issues of class and race. Third, she identified narratives with idealized and sentimental elements. Half of the six thousand narratives found by Starling came from antislavery periodicals, sources that could have been tampered with to embellish stories. The other half were in judicial records, broadsides, private printings, scholarly journals, church records, and the oral interviews referred to above. Starling's work gave voice to the Black slave, who before the 1940s was silenced. Out of respect for her family, who remained opposed to the subject of her research, Starling's important contribution remained unpublished for several decades. She agreed to publish the manuscript in 1981 when invited to become part of Yale's series in African American studies.

Marion Wilson Starling's academic excellence and activism continued throughout her life. She was appointed to the English Department at Brooklyn College in 1946 where she taught classes in Shakespeare, the Bible, and children's literature. She taught the first African American literature course in the department in 1954. Marion Wilson Starling's devotion to higher learning and to her colleagues led to her participation in leadership positions in the Professional Staff Congress, the faculty union. After retirement in 1982, Marion and her daughter, Tiffany, created an exhibit for the Hunter College Library titled *Blacks at Hunter, 1873–Present*. The exhibit identified several milestones demonstrating the inclusion of Black students, faculty, and alumni in the history of the college. Marion Wilson Starling died in 1994.

Hunter students of the 1920s remained committed to the dual challenges of academic excellence and activism promoted by President George S. Davis; by beloved faculty like Helen Gray Cone, E. Adelaide Hahn, Edna

Wells Luetz, Adele Bildersee, and Sarah Parks; and by student leaders like Mina Rees and Bella Visono Dodd. The Student Council established a regular Forum that invited speakers to address political and civic issues like racism and disarmament. Cognizant of the support they received from the city for free higher education, the Student Council sent a proposal to Congress urging the federal government to eliminate child labor, to enable all children to receive education to become thoughtful citizens. Capitalizing on their status as the largest women's college in the world, students asked for funding for a new building to meet their growing needs. Most graduates of the 1920s continued to serve New York as teachers, with some becoming school principals and others joining the faculty of their alma mater. Two outstanding graduates of the class of 1928, Edna Flannery Kelly and Marion Wilson Starling, made history. Kelly was the first Hunter graduate to serve in Congress. Starling made a significant contribution to scholarship with her research on slave narratives.

Chapter Three

A Turbulent Decade (1929–1939)

In February 1928, after twenty years at the helm, President Davis took a sabbatical leave of absence. On March 26, 1929, James M. Kieran, a longtime member of the faculty and dean of education, was installed as the third president of Hunter College, the largest college in New York City and the largest women's college in the world. In his inaugural address, Kieran stated that all colleges were faced with a twofold problem: the increasing number of students matriculating and the greater variety of work those students wanted to pursue. These issues were particularly true for Hunter College where day session student numbers had grown tenfold from 548 in 1908 to 5,500 in 1928. The summer session in 1928 registered 3,190. Evening session students grew to 7,772 that year. Hunter now offered the BA as well an MA in liberal arts, and a BS (bachelor of science) and MS (master of science) in education. Having outgrown the Park Avenue building, the college started offering freshman classes on Eighty-Fifth Street in 1926; the Brooklyn and Queens annexes were both started that year; the following year, the Thirty-Second Street annex was opened for freshmen and sophomores; and a new annex was added in 1929 on Twenty-Ninth Street.

President Kieran's inaugural address was printed in the March 1929 issue of the *Echo*. Kieran described problems that were created by the rapid growth of the student body. Some high school graduates who applied for admission to Hunter College were not prepared to do work at the collegiate level and he believed they should not be admitted. Some courses that students wished to study were in his view not of collegiate standard and should not become part of the Hunter curriculum. Kieran urged that a new type of post-high school program be created for such students and courses. These were new problems that had not been faced by Hunter's first two presidents. They would be perennial issues in future decades.

Kieran identified another new challenge faced by Hunter College. While 90 percent of the graduates entered the teaching profession, 10 percent pursued a liberal arts curriculum with no intention of teaching. With a population of almost six thousand students, hundreds would graduate with few job skills. Kieran believed that Hunter College must provide an education that would prepare those students to enter the world of business and commerce where jobs were increasing. He believed that the services of intelligent college women with special training, combined with a broad cultural background, were needed in the city and in the nation. Hunter College would strive to provide its graduates with the appropriate skills. He concluded his address with an observation: "The importance of the college graduate in the nation, and the position of the nation in international affairs have changed an ideal originally adopted mainly with the individual advantage in mind, into a matter of civic obligation." With this statement, President Kieran expanded the traditional idea of a liberal arts education to include a vast array of professional opportunities for women.

In 1930, to control the size of the incoming class, admissions requirements were raised. Fifteen units of high school work were now required: four years of English, one year of elementary algebra and one-half year of intermediate algebra, one year of plane geometry, one year of physics, chemistry, or advanced biology, one year of history, three years of a foreign language, two years of a second foreign language, and two and a half years of elective work approved by the admissions committee. In addition, a grade of 75 percent or better was required on Regent's tests in those subjects. In prior years, the required grade was 65 percent. To meet the needs of those who wished to seek employment in new fields, the college created a statistics major and a business major. It also created minor fields of study to complement majors. Students were encouraged to consider becoming teachers of accounting and of business, both new fields where jobs were plentiful. Similarly, courses in the psychology of the preschool child and in diagnostic testing and remedial teaching were introduced in response to job availability.

The new president was hopeful that the space problem would be solved during his tenure. Two of the planned five buildings to be constructed on the Bronx campus were scheduled to open in September 1930.

President Kieran saw the plans for a new campus as critical to the future of Hunter College. He reversed his predecessor's opposition to abandoning the Park Avenue building, now valued at $7 million, and encouraged the Board of Higher Education to continue to allocate funding for the new campus. Student interest in the project was keen. In the 1930 *Wistarion* students defined "Utopia" as the building plan for the Bronx campus. They dedicated the yearbook to Professor Lewis D. Hill for "storming City Hall with blueprints and visions of a perfect college."

The *Wistarion* of that year recognized several organizations for their efforts to support Hunter College and its students. Some were venerable, like the Alumnae Association, which had established new quarters at the Hotel Woodward at 204 West Fifty-Fifth Street. Mina Rees, the former Student Council president, now served as assistant recording secretary of the Association. In May, Marion Rhoads Elliott, president of the association, was sent as a delegate to the convention of the American Association of University Women held in Washington, DC. It was the first time that the Alumnae took an active part in the AAUW. The Alumnae Association completed fundraising for the Helen Gray Cone Fellowship Fund that spring.

Others, like the Judicial Board, were new organizations. The *Wistarion* boasted that the establishment of the board was another step in the direction of unifying the college and all its annexes, by bringing all students under the rule of one board with student representation from each class and faculty representation from each annex. Similarly, the freshman advisory system, established in 1929, replaced a system of direct communication between freshmen and juniors that was deemed no longer viable because students were assigned to different annexes. The growth in student numbers and in student activities also led to the publication of the *Freshman Handbook*, which was first printed in April 1929.

The circulating library, a new feature of Hunter College, managed by a student committee, specialized in current fiction. It had several hundred volumes of popular works of fiction, biography, and plays published within the last two years. Faculty, students, and clerical workers paid an annual membership fee of 50 cents and were entitled to withdraw books at 10 cents per week.

The Curriculum Committee, established in 1924, replaced the old system of student petitions to the faculty. It was designed to allow student ideas about the curriculum to be shared regularly with faculty. Committee members included faculty, alumnae, and students. For example, through the efforts of the Curriculum Committee and Il Circolo Italiano, the

Italian club, an Italian minor was established. The committee considered offering a course in Hebrew. This suggestion was sent to the Faculty Committee on Course of Study for further action. Classes in Hebrew were first offered in 1941.

During President Kieran's time, chapel was held on Wednesday mornings. No longer a daily event that included Bible readings, chapel remained a unifying factor of college life. Student Council business took over the agenda at several meetings each year. Musical chapels, featuring student performances, were popular. Well-known writers, lecturers, dancers, and others were invited. Martha Graham, modern dancer, choreographer, and founder of the Martha Graham Dance Company, performed at chapel. Phi Beta Kappa inductions were held annually at chapel and the names of new inductees were reported in the *Bulletin*.

The number of academic departments grew to sixteen in 1930. The faculty had grown to include 319 professors and 129 tutors and instructors. It remained largely female; many were graduates of Hunter. The continued presence of former students, now tutors, instructors, and professors, contributed to the feeling of connection held by current students to the Hunter of the past. In like manner, the regular participation of alumnae in college events and committees kept their ties to their alma mater strong. The *Bulletin* regularly reported on the achievements of recent graduates; *Echo* sometimes published poems or stories by alumnae; *Wistarion* periodically featured profiles of college leaders. Each of these elements contributed to the unique spirit of the college.

Students of the thirties were profoundly affected by the Depression. Some, like Sylvia Feldman (Porter), came from families that were ruined by the 1929 stock market crash. Sylvia's father, a doctor, died in 1925 when she was twelve. Her mother lost every penny the family had by speculating in the market before the crash. She was left with a home she couldn't sell and two cars she could neither sell nor drive as she had no money for gas. Sylvia's mother tried several jobs to support her family, finally becoming a successful milliner. Sylvia graduated from James Madison High School at sixteen and enrolled at Hunter College intending to become a novelist or a poet. However, her desire to understand what had happened to her family and to others suffering from sudden penury led her to study economics. Sylvia was a good student, was inducted into Phi Beta Kappa, and graduated *magna cum laude* in 1932. She married Reed R. Porter, a bank employee, shortly before graduation. Unable to obtain work because of the Depression and because she was a woman, she apprenticed at a new investment firm. Through this position and several other jobs on Wall Street, she acquired a broad financial understanding while taking graduate business classes at night at New York University. Using the byline S. F. Porter, to disguise her gender, as her employers did not want it known that she was a woman, she began to write articles for financial journals and a column for the *American Banker.*

The financial writing of the time was highly technical, incomprehensible to any but economists. Sylvia began using a different style in her financial advice columns for the *New York Evening Post* in 1935. Readers were receptive to her articles since they explained economic issues and injustices in terms they could understand. In 1938, the *Post* made her its financial editor, finally changing her byline in 1942 to Sylvia F. Porter, recognizing that her gender was an asset, not a liability. In 1944, Joan Robinson, a student, wrote a profile of Sylvia Porter in the *Echo*. She explained Sylvia's interest in economics: "At that time [the Depression] no curious person could help being interested in economics." Robinson noted that Sylvia was called "the girl wonder of Wall Street." In 1947 Sylvia's column became nationally syndicated, and she began to publish guidebooks on personal finance. Her columns appeared in 450 newspapers and reached forty million readers around the world. Sylvia F. Porter appeared on the cover of *Time* on November 28, 1960, noted as a trailblazer in the male-dominated field of finance.

Another student whose life was influenced by the Depression, Virginia Levitt (Snitow), graduated in 1931. Virginia was born in Brooklyn in 1911. Her father, Louis Levitt, was a member of the Workmen's Circle, a Jewish socialist organization. He sometimes took his daughter, aged eight, to meetings. Virginia remembered listening to speeches and to the discussions that followed. She didn't understand much, but she concluded that a meeting was an important place where people could talk and make things happen. Virginia excelled at her studies at Girls' High School in Brooklyn. She received a scholarship to attend art school but decided to follow her mother's advice to attend Hunter College. Tillie Levitt, like so many mothers of Hunter students, saw an independent future for her daughter as a teacher. Louis Levitt's dental practice began a long and steady decline during the Depression. Patients didn't come or didn't pay their bills. To economize, the family moved to 3312 Hull Avenue in the Bronx during Virginia's student years at Hunter.

Virginia's memory of the Workmen's Circle meetings was the catalyst that propelled her to join the History Club as a freshman. She recalled a student speaker from Spain who came to alert American college students to the struggle for freedom by Spanish students. She also remembered passionate discussions with classmates who sought solutions to the sufferings they witnessed close at hand. They debated and argued over lunch and in club meetings, addressing critical questions: What is socialism? How does it differ from communism? What is a dictatorship? Virginia reminisced:

> Looking back at my youth in the early '30s, I cannot imagine how we could have been so earnest, so hopeful, so innocent. The USSR was like a star of hope in the heavens, and Lincoln Steffens' stirring words: 'I have seen the future, and it works' sent ripples of hope and curiosity to the young people of my generation. We went through the miserable years of the Depression, the closing of the banks, the Dust Bowl refugees

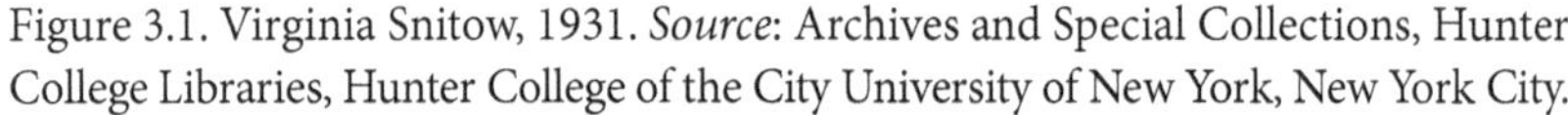
Figure 3.1. Virginia Snitow, 1931. *Source*: Archives and Special Collections, Hunter College Libraries, Hunter College of the City University of New York, New York City.

> from drought and lost farms with their whole lives piled up on rattletrap cars escaping to somewhere, out there.

Virginia's college years were filled with student activities. She was a member of the Journalism Club, participated in Varsity, in SING, and in Make-Up Box. She was vice president of the Student Council and a sorority sister in Phi Epsilon Epsilon. She was associate editor of the theater review, *Spotlight*. In her final year she took pedagogy classes and was a student teacher at the Model School (formerly the Normal College Training Department). Following graduation from Hunter, she took graduate courses in English literature at Columbia. In 1932, she began to teach at Wadleigh High School for Girls in Harlem; she remained on the faculty until 1944. In 1935 she married Charles Snitow, a lawyer and a trade show impresario.

Wadleigh High School, named for Lydia Wadleigh, the lady superintendent who had worked with Thomas Hunter in the early years of the Normal College, was established by the Board of Education in 1897 and moved into its new building in Harlem in September 1902. It was the first public high school for girls in New York City. (Hunter College High School did not become a separate entity until 1903.) Though the high school began with a largely Jewish student body, by the time Snitow arrived its students were primarily African American. Snitow's teaching record at Wadleigh was exemplary. Supervisors wrote glowing reviews of her work in the classroom. A report from June 1937 spoke of her work with students of different levels of ability: "Mrs. Snitow's program has ranged from the lowest to the highest. In all her work she continues to show initiative, resourcefulness, and thoroughness. Her attitude toward her pupils is especially friendly and understanding, yet her scholarly standards enable her to set sufficiently high standards of attainment for her classes. I consider her one of the most promising young teachers in the department." The supervisor went on to note that Snitow had become the faculty advisor of the school magazine, *Owl*, and that her work was distinguished.

Snitow's classes in the English Department and in pedagogy at Hunter were the foundation for her success in the classroom. Her experience in student clubs helped her to achieve success with the student newspaper at Wadleigh High School. But it was the informal college discussion groups that stimulated her desire to share her knowledge more broadly. In 1942, Snitow submitted an article to *The New Republic* titled "I Teach Negro

Girls." Published on November 9, 1942 and reissued a few months later in the *Negro Digest*, the article was a powerful description of what Snitow had learned from her pupils during the decade she taught at Wadleigh High School. "I arrived in Harlem with the usual luggage of preconceived notions, ready for anything among my students from mental inferiority to secret vice. . . . Classes from the first were quiet, the students friendly. When the first cracks appeared in the wall of reserve between us, I became aware of tension and resentment."

Snitow documented the challenges faced by her students by relating the following incident:

> It began one day when one of the Negro girls, a pretty, long-limbed creature, charming and constantly drowsy, fell sound asleep in my class. A few gentle snores gave her away. The class stopped a giggle in mid-career and watched me as if to say, "Well, what are you going to do about it?" Snitow hesitated. She was hurt and angry and walked down the aisle of desks to the sleeping student. "I looked down at the sprawled legs in torn stockings the high-heeled shoes which had been dyed black. I saw the delicate circles of weariness around her eyes and found myself saying somewhat helplessly to the class, 'What's the matter with her?' " A student responded: "She works all night. She's a cigarette girl." Snitow walked back to her desk and announced, "Let her sleep. She probably needs it."

That experience marked the beginning of Snitow's understanding that her students faced problems previously unknown to her.

In the article, Snitow reflected on the children of poverty and the ghetto. They were all different, but the pattern underlying their problems was the same. Knowing their actual circumstances, Snitow marveled at her neat and starched students who wrote compositions on inane topics like "The Family Car," "Home Decorating Is Fun," "Plans for a House Party." She also began to understand why some apparently bright, alert girls were frequently poor students. The world of Shakespeare and Milton, of Wordsworth and Burns was unreal and even meaningless to them. When she introduced discussions of Richard Wright's *Native Son*, of important figures of Negro history and culture, and of the Negro newspaper, *The People's Voice*, the students were animated and enthusiastic.

Snitow denounced the outmoded curriculum that denied her pupils knowledge of their history, pride in their traditions. "Ours is the blame that they are largely ignorant of their history and their heroes, their contributions to the society in which they live. We have given the Negro nothing but the remembrance of the shame of slavery. Studying in white man's textbooks, they see no reflection of their share in the glory of America, in man's immemorial struggle for liberty."

The teaching experience at Wadleigh radicalized Snitow. She became active in the New York Teachers Union and joined the Communist Party, traveling to the Soviet Union in 1936. She remained a party member until the mid-1940s when sectarianism beset the party. In later life Snitow became president of the Women's Division of the American Jewish Congress and led the organization to oppose American involvement in the Vietnam War. She participated in the Selma to Mongomery civil rights march in 1965 and three years later protested nuclear testing. In the 1980s Snitow became an advocate for women's rights in Israel and for women's studies programs in Israel and at Hunter College. She died in 2000.

During the Depression years, Hunter students like Porter and Snitow recognized that they were part of the larger world with its social, political, and economic problems. Student Council activities sought to make college life and thinking broader and more inclusive; a political symposium with student speakers representing Republican, Democratic, Communist, and Socialist parties was held late in October 1933. Student Council sent a delegate to the twenty-fifth annual meeting of the Women's Intercollegiate Press Conference. Delegates from Student Council were also sent to the Youth Conference Against War, held in New York City, and to the National Student Council against War, held in Chicago.

Hunter alumnae recognized the need to address unemployment among their members. While the Hunter Bureau of Occupations continued to respond to the needs of students for jobs, the alumnae committee pledged to find work for any graduate in need of a position. They identified and funded jobs at Hunter, in the library, and in laboratories. They also placed graduates in museum work and funded those positions too. One of the students who would benefit from this support was Pauli Murray who graduated in 1933 at the height of the Depression.

Anna Pauline (Pauli) Murray was born in Baltimore in 1910. She was three years old when her mother died. She was sent to live in Durham, North Carolina, with her aunt, Pauline, a teacher, and her maternal grandparents, Cornelia and Robert Fitzgerald. Cornelia had been born in bondage; her mother was part Cherokee, and her father was the owner's son. Robert was Black, raised in Philadelphia; he had fought for the Union during the Civil War. Pauli was a star pupil at Hillside High School. When she graduated at fifteen, she was the editor of the school newspaper, the president of the literary society, class secretary, a member of the Debate Club, a forward on the basketball team, and the top student. Whereas her friends planned to be stenographers, social workers, and teachers, she planned to study law. Her friends shortened their skirts. She wore only pants. Her teachers thought she should go to Wilberforce, a Black college in Ohio. They voted her a small scholarship to get her through her first semester. She turned it down as she wanted to go to New York City.

Aunt Pauline traveled with Pauli to Columbia University in the summer of 1926. There they discovered that Columbia did not accept women to their undergraduate college and that her credentials for Barnard were lacking several required classes. They also learned that Barnard charged $300 for tuition and $300 for room and board. Since Aunt Pauline earned only $970 a year as a teacher in a Black elementary school in Durham, attendance at Barnard was not possible. A Barnard dean advised Pauli to apply to Hunter where tuition was free. Pauli met with a dean at Hunter who explained that she needed additional high school classes to meet the admission standards. She also needed to establish residency in New York City. As a result, she went to live with relatives in Queens and enrolled in Richmond Hill High School, working hard to complete the missing credits. She spent the year following her second high school graduation back in Durham working as a janitor, a typist, a reporter, and finally as a stenographer to earn money to help with expenses when she returned to New York.

In September 1928, seventeen-year-old Pauli Murray returned to her family in Richmond Hill and began her freshman year in the Hunter annex in Brooklyn. She commuted one hour each way on the elevated train with many Hunter students who turned the train into a combination study hall and social center. One train friend, Pauline Diner, a Jewish girl (half the student body was then Jewish), tutored her in German. Pauline's help allowed Pauli to pass the required course with a "D." She also gained an appreciation for Jewish culture, attending her first Passover seder in Pauline's home.

Another friend, Lula Burton, the only other Black student in the Brooklyn annex, was in Pauli's English class. The class, taught by Professor

Catherine Reigart, proved a challenge to Pauli. Lula performed at a high level, but Pauli got a C- and D. Professor Reigart praised her originality, but faulted her poor grammar, stilted images, limited vocabulary, and apparent lack of general knowledge. Lula offered to help. Sitting with Pauli on the front steps of her house, Lula read aloud from the works of her favorite modern American poets—Edna St. Vincent Millay, Claude McKay, Countee Cullen, and Langston Hughes. Pauli began to imagine herself as part of a literary world in the making. Professor Reigart provided further encouragement when she invited both Pauli and Lula to her apartment for tea. Pauli marveled at its exotic décor, acquired in foreign travel, and delighted to hear her teacher speak about past adventures. Encouraged by her teacher's attention and her friend's help, Pauli redoubled her efforts. Her last paper on Grandfather Robert Fitzgerald earned an A–. Reigart praised her efforts: "You have a unique opportunity to influence a continent. . . . How proud I am to have had a small part in your education."

Pauli enjoyed further success in a political science course taught by Professor Elsa de Haas who insisted that students read the daily *New York Times* to broaden their understanding of the wider world. Pauli noted that the *Times* spelled Negro with a capital "N," which boosted her racial confidence. She began to use Negro and colored interchangeably. Pauli later reflected on the Hunter spirit: "Hunter's tradition for excellence was so strong that in later years I was surprised to find how often I could recognize a Hunter-trained woman by the thoroughness with which she approached her work."

In the spring of her freshman year Pauli left Richmond Hill and moved to the Emma Ransom residence at the West 137th Street YWCA in Harlem, where a cousin, Susie Elliot, was director. From the window in her fourth-floor room, Pauli could see the Abyssinian Baptist Church and hear the music from the choir and organ. She borrowed a bicycle from the recreation director and rode all over the city. To earn rent money, Pauli worked at the switchboard and in the cafeteria. She loved Harlem. In Brooklyn and Queens her brown skin set her uncomfortably apart, but in Harlem she saw Blacks everywhere. With its ninety thousand migrants from the American South, the Caribbean, and other countries, it was the capital of Black America, home to the greatest outpouring of African American art, literature, and music in history.

During the summer of 1929, Pauli left her job at the YWCA for a better paying job at the Alice Foote MacDougall restaurant on West Forty-Sixth St. She worked five-hour shifts, six nights a week, for $4.00

plus tips. She resented the fact that the restaurant hired Black waitresses but served only whites. Once, when a Black couple was refused service, the entire staff walked out. As a further indignity, the staff was not allowed to order from the menu; they were offered leftovers in the basement. Pauli kept her job for several months, using her extra money to attend cultural events—*The Merchant of Venice* at the Shubert Theater, *Richelieu* at Hampden's Theater, *Tristan und Isolde* at the Metropolitan Opera, the Fisk University Choir at Carnegie Hall, and the Hall Johnson Negro Choir at Town Hall.

The stock market crash of 1929 led to the end of her waitressing job and made it harder for her to make ends meet. Pauli took up smoking and lost fifteen pounds during her sophomore year at Hunter. In October 1930 she learned through the YWCA employment office about a full-time job at Open Road, a travel agency at 20 West Forty-Third Street. The ad was for an "intelligent colored girl" to work as a switchboard operator and stenographer for $20 a week. This agency organized tours to the Soviet Union. A business that arranged tours to the Soviet Union needed to demonstrate lack of racial prejudice. Pauli got the job and married William Roy Wynn a month later, keeping the marriage secret so that Pauli could keep her room at the Y. They spent a week in a cheap West Side hotel. The marriage, which was later annulled, was a brief, painful episode. Pauli, who had always been a "tomboy," was conflicted about her identity as a woman. Without the words to describe her feelings, she explored a nonbinary existence.

In February 1931 she registered for classes but dropped out after a few weeks. Pauli and a friend, Dorothy Hayden, dressed as Boy Scouts, with close-cropped hair, and decided to hitchhike across the country. They were picked up by the Traveler's Aid Society in Bridgeport and were returned to New York City. Pauli set off again in April with a friend of Dorothy's who was driving to Northern California. They followed US Route 30. Pauli wrote a poem, "The Song of the Highway." In California, she received a note from Aunt Pauline, who was ill and wanted her to come home immediately. Having no money, Pauli dressed as a man and rode the rails. She made it home to Durham where she learned that her aunt had improved and quickly headed back to New York City.

In September 1931, she returned to Hunter, taking classes at the main campus on Park Avenue. She had lost a year and was determined to graduate in three semesters. She went to the employment bureau and landed a part-time clerical job in the journalism office that paid $6 a week. She was also helped with a clothing contribution that kept her warm for the coming year. Pauli was required to commit to a major at the beginning of her junior year. She considered history, but she hated the yearlong course in American history she took that year. Her grandfather and teachers in Hillside High School had made her love history and appreciate the role that African Americans played in fostering public education and other democratic institutions in the post–Civil War South. At Hunter, she was taught the standard account, that Blacks, because they were less evolved than whites, had held the South back. Losing interest, she got C's both semesters.

The social science class she liked was an introduction to anthropology taught by Dorothy L. Keur, a *summa cum laude* alumna of Hunter, class of 1925, with an MA from Columbia, who was only five years her senior. Keur, having studied with Franz Boas and Ruth Benedict, presented a positive perspective on Pauli's multiracial background. Keur required her students to visit the Hall of Man at the American Museum of Natural History each week. There, Pauli found models of villages from around the world that displayed the variety of human experience within specific cultural contexts. She was particularly affected by the portrayal of African and Native American peoples; here were the two streams of her ancestry displayed in the same positive light as Western European villagers.

Thinking that she wanted to be a writer, Pauli joined the Journalism Club, became a stringer for a Black newspaper, *The New York Age*, and won admission to Hunter's coveted English major and to the national English honor society, Sigma Tau Delta. As an English major, Pauli worked with some of the most talented Hunter students. Ruth M. Goldstein in particular inspired Pauli. As editor of *Echo*, Goldstein published Pauli's first article, "A Working Student," a slightly fictionalized account of her struggle to work and go to classes. Pauli began her essay with numerical data; of the 900 entering students in 1932, 330 intended to work while they were in college, 125 partially supported themselves, and 7 were wholly self-supporting. She concluded from this survey that there were three distinct classes of students at Hunter: those who do not work outside of school, those who work part-time to defray some expenses, and those who must earn their living while in school.

Pauli belonged to the last group. She described the long hours of poorly paid work that led to her exhaustion in class. Her routine of alternately sleeping and waking, struggling to finish assignments, had led to an involuntary loss of fifteen pounds and low blood pressure. She was

Figure 3.2. Pauli Murray, 1933. *Source*: Archives and Special Collections, Hunter College Libraries, Hunter College of the City University of New York, New York City.

embarrassed by not having money to pay club dues, school fees, or for student papers and magazines. Nevertheless, Pauli averred, her experience prepared her to face life's many problems. She learned how to take advantage of every opportunity. Pauli graduated in January 1933, one of four Black women in the midyear graduating class of 232 women.

Unable to find full-time employment, she was happy to get a job running the Hunter switchboard in the evenings. She was the first Black alumna to hold this job, which paid $11 a week. While working there she wrote "Youth, 1933" and "The Newer Cry," poems that conveyed her conflicted feelings about her place in the world. In the first she celebrated young communists from Harlem to Berlin—"Armed with red banners, placards, and worthless diplomas . . . perched on soapboxes, platforms and ladders." It exhorted all who stopped to "Read it, Comrade, and join the Movement!" The second was an expression of racial identity. She worried that white youths did not appreciate the dangers of violence as much as their Black counterparts did. "Man is a slave only to himself," she wrote, not convinced that the larger social structure was to blame for the condition.

In the fall of 1933, Pauli landed a new job selling subscriptions to *Opportunity*, the journal of the National Urban League. Though she was now earning $15 a week, the job involved a lot of travel, leading to health problems. Pauli was diagnosed with pleurisy and prescribed a long rest. She was sent to Camp Tera, a racially integrated convalescent camp for women not far from New York City where she had months of rigorous outdoor exercise and good food. Pauli gained weight and lost her cough. When she returned to New York City, she was hired by the Works Progress Administration, a New Deal program to provide employment. She taught remedial reading at P.S. 8, south of Greenwich Village, earning $23.86 a week, the most she had ever earned. Simultaneously, she took courses at the New Workers' School in Marxist philosophy and historical materialism.

Pauli's relatives in Durham urged her to return home. Worried about her family and lacking job prospects, Murray applied to the University of North Carolina for graduate work in sociology. The response she received was brief: "Members of your race are not admitted to the University." Pauli asked the NAACP to represent her in a lawsuit, but they declined, feeling that her status as a New York resident would jeopardize the case. In March 1940, Murray invited a friend to go home to Durham with her for Easter. The young Black women traveled south by bus. When they changed buses in Richmond, Virginia, segregated seating rules required the friends to sit in the back of the bus. Since the only available seats in the back were broken, they sat in the last row of the seats reserved for white passengers. The bus driver demanded that they move. When they refused, he called the police, who charged the two women with disorderly conduct. They were found guilty and fined $43. Not having any money, they spent several days in jail.

Murray returned to New York and worked for the Workers Defense League. She was asked to raise money on behalf of Odell Waller, a Virginia sharecropper who had been sentenced to death for shooting the white man whose land he farmed. Waller claimed he shot in self-defense. The prosecution claimed he killed in cold blood. Murray went to Richmond to raise funds. Civil rights lawyer and founder of the NAACP Legal Defense Fund Thurgood Marshall and Howard law professor Leon Ranson attended her talk and were impressed by her logic. Ranson urged her to apply to Howard Law School and promised her a scholarship.

In September 1941 Murray enrolled at Howard Law School, the only woman in her class. On the first day, one of her professors announced that he didn't know why a woman would want to go to law school. Murray felt humiliated and simultaneously determined to become the top student. She called discrimination against Black women "Jane Crow." In July 1942, Murray worked with Maida Springer of the International Ladies' Garment Workers' Union and Dollie Lowther of the Laundry Workers' Union to stage a peaceful march in Washington to protest lynching, Jim Crow, and the poll tax.

After receiving her JD, Murray applied to Harvard for further graduate work and received the following letter: "You are not of the sex entitled to be admitted to Harvard Law School." She went to Berkeley instead, passed the California bar exam in 1945, and then returned to New York to look for a job. At the time, very few law firms hired women, and especially not Black women. She scraped by on low-paying jobs until 1948 when the women's division of the Methodist Church asked her to do a survey of the legal requirements for segregation in the thirty-one states where they had parishes. Murray produced a 746-page book, *States' Laws on Race and Color*, that exposed the extent of American segregation. The ACLU distributed copies to law libraries, Black colleges, and human rights organizations.

It took her several years to pass the bar exam in New York, as she encountered questioning of her possible affiliation with communists during the character interview. Disappointed and discouraged, Murray turned to writing her family history. She saw herself as a mixed-race, mixed-class, mixed-gendered person, doomed to failure, but she kept writing. Pauli had written her first story about Grandfather Robert Fitzgerald for her English class at Hunter. While operating the Hunter switchboard she wrote another story, "American Credo," about her grandfather's contribution to the Civil War, his commitment to education and to civil rights, and his loyalty to America. She continued to write family stories and published them in a book, *Proud Shoes*, in 1956. The book came out two years after the Supreme Court decided *Brown v. Board of Education*, overturning *Plessy v. Ferguson*. The winning argument relied on the prohibition against separate conditions in the Thirteenth and Fourteenth Amendments to the Constitution. Murray had used this very argument in her final papers at

Howard. Professor Ranson brought her ideas, for which she is now well known, to the attention of those arguing the case.

Her professional career continued at Paul, Weiss, Rifkind, Wharton & Garrison, a progressive firm with more than sixty lawyers where Murray was the only Black and one of only three women. In 1960, Pauli spent a year in Ghana teaching law and then went to Yale to study for a PhD in law. In April 1961, Eleanor Roosevelt wrote to ask her to serve on a Presidential Commission on the Status of Women; she agreed. Murray addressed the commission, stating that the struggle for civil rights for Blacks and the struggle for civil rights for women were inherently similar. She proposed using the Fourteenth Amendment as an avenue to secure women's rights to avoid the controversy between those who supported the Equal Rights Amendment and those who wanted to maintain protective labor legislation for women. Murray argued, "The Court had permitted a policy originally directed toward the protection of a segment of a woman's life to dominate and inhibit her mature development as an individual."

On June 14, 1965, Pauli Murray became the first Black person to receive the JSD, the doctor of juridical science degree, at Yale. Three years later she was offered a faculty position at Brandeis, earning $20,000. The following year she joined a dozen professors around the US who had begun to experiment with courses in women's history. Her course was based on the vantage point of Black women. Five years later she resigned her position and became a student at the General Theological Seminary in New York City. She was among the first generation of women priests and the first African American ordained an Episcopal priest in January 1977. She died in July 1985.

In 1933, President Kieran, who had presided over the graduations of Sylvia Feldman (Porter), Virginia Levitt (Snitow), and Anna Pauline (Pauli) Murray, announced his decision to retire. He had spent thirty years at Hunter and had supervised the education and training of half the elementary school teachers in the city and one third of the principals. During his brief tenure, President Kieran announced one small change to long-standing college custom that had a lasting impact on the college. He addressed the understanding that any woman on the faculty must resign from her position upon marriage. As a result, women on the Hunter College faculty had remained single. Kieran, whose wife and daughters were Hunter alumnae, announced that married women were welcome to stay; they had only to inform the payroll office of their name change.

This new policy led to expanded career opportunities for many women professors at Hunter College.

On May 16, 1933, Eugene A. Colligan, who held a bachelor of science degree from Teachers College and a PhD from Fordham, was installed as the fourth president of Hunter College. In his inaugural address, Colligan explained that changing times necessitated changes to the Hunter College experience:

> The democratization of the higher education of women in this whirling world of changed economic, social and political conditions, together with improved educational methods and ideas demands of us vision and growth. Education must aim at something more than merely the filling of minds with the things a cultured person ought to know and learn from our custodians of learning. . . . The main point of all educational reform is to find and serve individual pupil capacity. Only on this basis, in a democracy which promises equality of opportunity, can educational standards and curricula have meaning and vitality.

These sentiments were a celebration of the individual and ignored the college culture with its tradition of student activism for the common good. President Colligan was soon embroiled in controversy as he moved to put an end to Hunter students' participation in the national student peace movement. But Hunter students were firm in their beliefs. Committed to the ethos of *Mihi cura futuri* as well as the dual qualities of excellence and activism established in previous decades, Hunter students were inspired by the antiwar movement. The chapel held on March 28, 1934, was devoted to introducing an antiwar conference planned for the next day. The Peace Council of the college had been studying the economic causes of war, the international munitions business, the role of the press in war propaganda, and the part labor unions might play in opposition to war and urged the student body and faculty to attend the conference.

Colligan informed the students that specific resolutions would not be tolerated at their conference. He deprived them of a meeting place on campus and assigned faculty to supervise their activities. Following the conference, Colligan met with a small group of students and faculty, warning that the control of an organized minority over student affairs would have to be ended or the Student Council would be dissolved. One week later, he dissolved the Student Council and placed faculty advisors in charge of all clubs and publications. The Peace Council, spearhead of antiwar agitation, was also abolished.

These actions led to spontaneous widespread revolt. The Student Council condemned the actions as a complete nullification of student self-government. The Peace Council refused to acknowledge its dissolution and asserted its right to exist. The *Bulletin* published a special issue on March 1, 1935, with the headline "Students Protest the Nunan Bill!" This bill required all students in New York State to take an oath to support the Constitution of the United States and the Constitution of the State of New York. Hunter students joined the National Student Federation of America, the National Student League, and the Student League for Industrial Democracy in a move to defeat the bill. Jean Ford, editor of the *Bulletin*, joined the editors of student newspapers at City College of New York, Columbia, New York University, and Fordham on a trip to Albany to protest the bill. On March 11, the *Bulletin* reported that seventy-five hundred students from thirteen colleges protested the bill.

On April 11, the day before a nationwide student strike for peace was scheduled, the Peace Council invited a representative from the Women's League for Peace and Freedom to address them. As she began to speak a representative of President Colligan interrupted the meeting, demanding that the speaker meet with the president in his office. Several students accompanied her to the president's office. They were told to wait outside and refused. Two of the student leaders were suspended. Despite these actions, the following day twenty-two hundred students, denied a meeting place on campus, met in midtown. Two hundred of them marched to President Colligan's office to present a resolution condemning the suspensions. Colligan responded in anger: "I will not be dictated to by any group of students." The following day three additional students received letters informing them that they had been suspended.

Detectives were assigned to the campus. When the Peace Council met on April 30, Dean Hannah Egan entered the meeting accompanied by two policemen. The speaker, Joseph Cadden, a leader of the American Student Union, was escorted by the dean to the president's office. The police remained with the students until the dean returned and took down some names of those in the room and dismissed them. Colligan's reprisals against students resorted to slander. He told a group of parents that he possessed nauseating facts about the private lives of the suspended students. On May 16, another session of the Peace Council met behind a door where the leaders had posted a sign: "This is NOT Nazi Germany. . . . Peace Council WILL MEET TODAY." Nevertheless, the meeting was invaded by police and its speaker forcibly removed from the building.

Hunter faculty supported the continued freedom of the Student Council in a front-page article in the *Bulletin*, implicitly rebuking President Colligan. Bella Visono Dodd, an alumna and faculty member, was invited to speak by the International Club. She gave a fiery speech to a packed auditorium, supporting peace and denouncing the path to war caused by imperialism, nationalism, and a disruption in the balance of power. Neither faculty nor students were intimidated by the actions of President Colligan.

Student involvement in mobilizations for peace continued in the mid-thirties. The Student Council sent delegates to the National Student Federation of America convention in Kansas City and to the convention of the American Student Union in Columbus, Ohio. Hunter student activists fought to maintain their rights to self-governance and their commitment to political protest. They mapped the history of self-governance and the wisdom they had gained from the process in the *Wistarion*:

> Many years ago . . . Hunter students were granted the right to govern themselves, with a view to teaching them how to face the problems which, in later life, would require of each individual, in their solution, an equal measure of self-control and self-government. . . . Lately, the students have found themselves confronted with a new problem, that of choosing judiciously between the many forces growing up in a discontented world. They have endeavored to meet this by showing always a truly academic attitude in permitting not only the vociferous but also the inarticulate to present a viewpoint on these new world interests. They have realized that these interests must break into the campus life, because that campus life is but a preparation for the world. . . . They have learned that he who yells the loudest is not always right, that there may be motives behind proposals that do not appear on the surface. With this judicial attitude the Student Administration will always try to maintain the balance between the right and the left, as it has from its origin, as a guide to the opinions and actions of the six-thousand-odd Hunter students.

Despite their judicious language, Colligan did not permit the editors of the 1935 *Wistarion* to use photographs of students protesting in their yearbook. Instead, the editors wrote proudly about the unique nature of the Hunter student body:

> Hunter students are cosmopolitan. A Hunter student knows of race prejudice and bigotry only through her studies. In the college halls one meets fellow students of every turn of life, who were born in every corner of the globe, whose parents are occupied in every imaginable pursuit. . . . The most truly educative property of Hunter is this varied background of its members, which broadens and strengthens the students and makes them more fit to make the contacts of their chosen careers. For this reason, we may say, "This is a Hunter student, not only the embodiment of youth but also of open-mindedness and human understanding."

Hunter faculty, many of whom were alumnae, stood with the students as they continued to act out their beliefs in opposition to President Colligan. College records are silent about the guidance Colligan may have received from the Board of Trustees at this time.

One student who was representative of the cosmopolitan nature of Hunter in the thirties achieved a leadership role in the college. The *Wistarion* profiled Soia Mentschikoff, Student Council president 1933–1934, who explained that her chief task "was to present the students' views to the new administration." Based on the robust activities of the Student Council and the Peace Council that it supported, Soia fulfilled her mission more than adequately. The *Bulletin* announced an award given to Soia by the alumnae of 1878, proving that the alumnae supported her actions. The award paid for her first year of graduate studies.

Born in 1915 in Moscow to a branch of the storied Mentschikoff family of Russian nobility, Soia grew up after the Russian Revolution of 1917, on the Upper West Side. At Hunter she majored in political science, was captain of the basketball team, played hockey, and chaired publicity for SING. After graduating from Hunter in 1934, she attended law school at Columbia, receiving her degree in 1937. She was best known for her work developing the Uniform Commercial Code, a set of laws governing all commercial transactions in the United States, including the sale and lease of all goods, banking transactions, and investment securities. In 1947,

Figure 3.3. Soia Mentschikoff, front row, second from right, and Student Council, 1934. *Source*: Archives and Special Collections, Hunter College Libraries, Hunter College of the City University of New York, New York City.

she was the first woman hired to teach at Harvard Law School. She taught for two decades at the University of Chicago Law School and was later the dean of the University of Miami School of Law. She died in June 1984.

Another member of the class of 1934 who added to the cosmopolitan nature of Hunter College was Belle (Bel) Kaufman. Born in Berlin in 1911, where her father was studying medicine, she returned with her family to Odessa, growing up in a "city of poets and sailors, merchants and musicians, Jewish intellectuals, and exotic strangers from the Black Sea." During the Russian Revolution the family fled to Berlin and arrived in the United States in 1923. Belle's native language was Russian; she spoke French and German. But she knew no English when she arrived in New York at the age of twelve. She was enrolled in a first-grade class with six year olds and was helped to learn English by her teachers. Belle attended high school in New Jersey and completed her first year of college at New York University. She entered Hunter College in 1931 as a sophomore, having established New York City residency.

One of her extracurricular activities was the Journalism Club. Belle was assigned to the *Bronx Home News*. Journalism Club was the only activity for which students were paid; the longer the piece, the larger the check. Belle interviewed her close friend Joy Davidman, who was one of the youngest in her class. Joy mentioned that she was not dating anyone at the time and that she was studying Latin. Belle's story appeared on the first page of the second section of the *Bronx Home News* with a photo and the caption "Shuns Cupid for Classics." Belle was called to the office of Dean Egan for failing to clear the article and the caption with Emma K. Temple, her faculty advisor. Belle admitted her failure to follow the rules. Dean Egan continued, "And you know, Joy's father is a high school principal and that is a very damaging." Before she could finish, Joy arrived, announcing that her father was delighted with the article and the issue was dropped. Belle was not expelled, but for a moment she was frightened.

Belle became secretary of the English Club, and a member of Make-Up Box and the Shakespeare Society. Her stories were published in the *Echo*. Her best friends were Elizabeth MacDougal and Margaret Grennan. MacDougal was Black. One day, Belle called at Elizabeth's home and was surprised when the door was opened by a Black man. It was obviously her father, but it had not occurred to Belle that Elizabeth was Black; she was just Elizabeth. Margaret Grennan was a fellow English major. Belle's friends encouraged her to enroll in an education class. Her family were all writers. Her grandfather was the famous novelist Sholem Aleichem, who published in Yiddish. Her mother published over two thousand short stories. Her father, a physician, was also a translator and poet. Belle's experience student teaching convinced her to become a teacher. She graduated *magna cum laude*. She enrolled as a graduate student in English at Columbia, specializing in the eighteenth century, and received her MA with highest honors in 1936. She was offered a doctoral fellowship but declined in order to support her husband in medical school by teaching.

Belle worked as a substitute teacher for many years in different schools. She began to submit short stories to *Esquire*, changing her first name to Bel, thinking it less obviously a female name as the magazine did not yet publish anything by women. In November 1962 she sent an article to *The Saturday Review of Literature* titled "From a Teacher's Wastebasket." Composed of spoken dialogue, letters, memoranda, notes, formal circulars, student tests, and compositions, the work was a humorous look at the endless memos and forms she had been asked to complete. She was immediately offered a book contract to expand the article, which was published three years later as *Up the Down Staircase*. It was a great success, ultimately selling six million copies in sixteen languages, and was made into a popular movie in 1967.

On December 7, 1987, Bel accepted an invitation from the Soviet Embassy to join Russian leader Mikhail Gorbachev as his guest at a reception held for prominent Americans. She participated in the Moscow International Forum where she delivered a speech on "The Role of Culture in Protecting Civilization and Universal Human Values." She continued to teach and write through the end of the century. A celebration of Bel's one hundredth birthday was held at Roosevelt House. Bel died in Manhattan in 2014, at age 103.

Like many of her classmates, Lucy Schildkret (Dawidowicz) was a student who arrived at Hunter College with strong feelings about her future. Born in 1915 in New York City to Polish immigrant parents, Schildkret attended Hunter College High School. In her senior yearbook she wrote: "Nothing bigger can come to a being than to love a great cause and work for it." During her years at Hunter College, from 1932 to 1936, she majored in English and participated actively in the publication of the *Echo*. She joined its literary staff in May 1934, became associate editor in May 1935, and editor-in-chief in November 1935. Lucy's first publication was a short story, "Romance"; this was followed by four poems. The last one, "In Memoriam: 1917," published in May 1936, reveals her strong feelings about war and peace:

> Lost generation, victim of oratory and defective machine,
> Pressed by panic and platitudes. Under open-sky terror,
> Night blotted out by walls of flame,
> And disemboweled bodies:
> These the remnants of memory
> To plague their days and nights . . .
> Their blame
> For the unheard prophet's cry:
> "Gentlemen, if you want peace,
> Disarm!"

Lucy Schildkret struggled to find employment following graduation. She worked part-time at Macy's and searched for something meaningful to do. Lucy enrolled in graduate courses in English at Columbia and in graduate courses in Jewish history at Mitlshul, a Yiddish language and culture school. Jacob Shatzky, who was one of Lucy's history professors at Mitlshul, asked if she had considered studying Jewish history. He proposed a research topic, the Yiddish press in England. Her advisor at Columbia approved the topic. As her work progressed, Shatzky suggested that she go to Vilna to study at the Yiddish Scientific Institute (YIVO). Schildkret went to Vilna in August 1938 and returned to New York thirteen months later where she worked for the American branch of YIVO. In 1945 she returned to Columbia to study Jewish history with Professor Salo W. Baron; she was awarded an MA in 1946. In January 1948, having spent fifteen months in Displaced Persons camps interviewing Holocaust survivors in Germany, Lucy married a survivor, Szymon Dawidowicz. Twenty years later, teaching Jewish history at Stern College and at the Wurzweiler School of Social Work of Yeshiva University, she created the first university course in the US on the history of the Holocaust. In 1975, she published *The War Against the Jews*, which became the standard book on the Holocaust for many years and continues to be used in classes today. Lucy Dawidowicz died in 1990.

While Lucy Schildkret Dawidowicz flexed her writerly muscles as a Hunter student, Beatrice Brown, who immigrated to New York from Leeds, England, at the age of four in 1922, was a musical presence at the college. Brown's mother gave her a violin and encouraged her musical interest. At sixteen she entered Hunter College where she was elected president of the Music Club and served in that capacity for all eight semesters of her student experience. During her senior year she studied viola and played as a member of a string quartet. While an undergraduate, she founded and directed the Hunter College Symphony Orchestra, elevating it to professional standards and performing in Town Hall concerts. Following her graduation in 1937, Brown taught in the Music Department and conducted the Hunter orchestra as well as the Gilbert and Sullivan Society for six years. In 1941 she cofounded the Young American Symphony Orchestra with Erno Rapee, presenting concerts with opera singers Jan Peerce and Regina Resnik, another Hunter graduate.

She received her MA in musicology at NYU and completed course work for her PhD at Columbia. Brown lived in Germany from 1953 to 1959, having received both Fulbright and Rockefeller grants to support her continuing study, the only woman to have received both awards. In 1962 she was hired by the Scranton Philharmonic Orchestra. *The New York Times* reported that she was the only woman under contract as a regular conductor in the East, and one of the few women holding a conductor's post. Brown continued to perform as a solo violist, often with Leopold Stokowski's American Symphony Orchestra. From 1970 until her death in 1997 Brown was the conductor of the Ridgefield Orchestra in Connecticut where she remained committed to performing music by contemporary American composers.

In addition to students of immigrant backgrounds, Hunter had a group of students interested in learning more about Black history and culture in the thirties. Though there were only one hundred Black students among the five thousand enrolled at Hunter, the group was determined to establish a new club to affirm their heritage and to study their contributions to national and world history and culture. In 1936, they established the Toussaint L'Ouverture Society, named for the Haitian general, born a slave, who led the Haitian Revolution, resisted Napoleon's order to restore slavery in Saint-Domingue, and died in a French prison in 1803. The Toussaint Society sponsored annual concerts and brought prominent speakers to campus. Dr. Willis H. Huggins, the first Black to receive a PhD from Fordham, and a dedicated scholar of African history, was invited to speak on "the history of the Negro," tracing it back to the kings of ancient Egypt and through to the present ruler of Ethiopia. His presentation offered a wealth of material on the contributions of Blacks to world history. The club offered a prize of $25 for the best essay on the contributions of the Negro to American history. Miriam Panger won the competition in 1939 with her essay, "The Negro and the Reconstruction Era." On December 20, 1938, the Student Council proposed and passed the following motion: "Student Council should support Toussaint L'Ouverture in its campaign to institute a course in Negro Culture and History."

On February 14, 1936, student and faculty interest in national and world events was abruptly diverted by a four-alarm fire that destroyed the main Hunter building on Park Avenue. Faculty, students, and alumnae turned their attention to the immediate crisis of finding temporary space for classes and to lobbying the Board of Higher Education for funds to rebuild in Manhattan.

Unlike his predecessor, President Colligan had no intention of closing the Park Avenue campus of the college. The board resolution to sell the site had remained in abeyance for several years. Hence, the deteriorating Park Avenue campus continued to function until the fire. Temporary quarters were quickly located for Hunter College and the Model School. Hunter College High School remained on East Ninety-Sixth Street. President Colligan rallied support from faculty, alumnae, and students to rebuild

Figure 3.4. Student Council discussion, 1932. *Source*: Archives and Special Collections, Hunter College Libraries, Hunter College of the City University of New York, New York City.

the Park Avenue campus. The Student Council presented petitions with eight thousand signatures to the board and worked with alumnae to gain support from influential organizations throughout the city.

Eight months after the fire, Eleonore Funk Hahn, a graduate of the class of 1875, presented a resolution to the New York City Federation of Women's Clubs meeting at the Hotel Astor. An overwhelming majority of the delegates voted to support the resolution, which read:

> Whereas, the traditional and time-hallowed location in Manhattan is an ideal one to meet the College's needs both old and new, because of its accessibility from all parts of the city, and its proximity to museums, libraries, Central Park, and the business section of the metropolis; therefore
>
> Be it resolved, that we, the New York City Federation of Women's Clubs in convention assembled, urge the construction at the earliest possible moment of centralized suitable buildings in the Borough of Manhattan for Hunter College;
>
> Be it further resolved, that we strongly recommend as a site for Hunter College the present eminently suitable one, namely the block bounded by Park and Lexington Avenues, 68th and 69th Streets, Manhattan, which is owned by the City and occupied by Hunter College.

Four months later, President Colligan addressed New Yorkers on WMCA radio to garner support for rebuilding: "Despite the grave handicaps imposed by inadequate and unsuitable buildings and the limitation of proper facilities for academic work, Hunter College today stands as a leader in progressive education among the colleges of the country." He pointed to recent curricular revisions that gave students a full liberal arts program as well as opportunities to specialize in four new fields: business, social service, pre-medical study, and journalism. He reminded listeners that more than thirty thousand Hunter graduates had brought their skills to the city, state, and nation, singling out the thousands of graduates who taught in public schools. He ended with a plea for the community to support the Board of Higher Education in its request to the Board of Estimate and Apportionment to include in the 1937 capital outlay budget $4,652,000 for the construction, furnishing, and equipping of a new Hunter College building on the old college site. He ended his appeal with a strong statement: "Our students and their parents, our staff and our alumnae are united in the earnest hope that promptly there will be erected on the site of the original building at Sixty-Eighth Street a suitable structure, worthy of the high academic standing and traditions of Hunter College, worthy of the womanhood of this municipality and worthy of the greatness of the City of New York, Wonder city of this Western World. We measure the progress of civilization by the way it treats its women."

In April 1937, in a reversal of his previous policy, President Colligan announced that he would participate in a meeting to be held by the Peace Council. His explanation of this change of policy was weak: "Our students, through sustained study for several years, have evidenced an abiding interest in the promotion of world peace." It's possible that the support he received from alumnae and students following the fire influenced his thinking. Colligan also approved changing the bell schedule to permit widespread participation in a peace strike organized by the Student Council. The students reiterated their concerns: to recognize the validity of the Oxford Oath, composed by students at Oxford University and adopted by students around the world. The oath was a promise to defend civil rights and academic freedom whose suppression is the first step toward fascism, and to recognize that fascism breeds war. Despite this change in policy, Colligan's term as president remained marked by his earlier authoritarianism.

Gertrude Elion, one of two Hunter alumnae to have been awarded a Nobel Prize, graduated *summa cum laude* with a major in biochemistry and a minor in physics a year after the fire, in 1937. The daughter of Eastern European immigrants, she was born in New York City in 1918. Her father was a dentist who had lost all his savings in the crash of 1929. Gertrude lived in the Bronx as a child, passing many hours at the Bronx Zoo. Gertrude was an excellent student who explained in her Nobel Prize acceptance speech that she would not have been able to attend college if she had to pay tuition. She entered Hunter College in 1933 and decided to major in science, motivated by the death of her grandfather who had succumbed to cancer when Gertrude was fifteen.

She remembered her Hunter days as very challenging and full of lively camaraderie among the students. Due to her straitened financial circumstances, she was unable to go on to graduate school, having not received a fellowship. Jobs were scarce and the few that existed in laboratories were not open to women. By 1939, she had saved some money and entered graduate school in chemistry at NYU, the only woman in her class. After a year of graduate studies, she had finished all the required courses but needed to do research for her MA degree. During the day, she taught high school chemistry, physics, and general science, and did her research at night. In 1941 she received her MA degree.

Following US entry into World War II and the drafting of thousands of men, Elion was able to get a job working in a laboratory, assigned to analytical quality control for a major food company. Two years later she began to work as an assistant to George Hitchings at a pharmaceutical company, Burroughs Wellcome, moving from organic chemistry to microbiology. Her horizons expanded to include biochemistry, pharmacology, immunology, and virology. From 1960 she was associated with the National Cancer Institute and with Burroughs Wellcome. Gertrude Elion shared the Nobel Prize in Physiology or Medicine in 1988 with George Hitchings and Sir James Black for their work in innovative drug design. She was the second Hunter alumna to win this award. (See chapter 4 for discussion of Rosalyn Yalow.) Elion and Hitchings had collaborated since 1945. They demonstrated the differences in nucleic acid metabolism between normal human cells, cancer cells, protozoa, bacteria, and viruses. They developed a series of drugs that block nucleic acid synthesis in cancer and noxious organisms without damaging normal human cells. This led them to develop drugs to fight leukemia, malaria, and herpes. Elion continued to do research until her death in 1999. She was also a loyal Hunter alumna, serving as a trustee of the Hunter College Foundation, was named as a member of the Hunter Hall of Fame, and was the recipient of both an honorary doctorate and a President's Medal from the college. In 2002, an endowed chair in chemistry was named in the Chemistry Department in her honor.

In 1938, responding to a reduced demand for teachers in the public school system in New York City, because of the continuing effects of budget shortfalls due to the Depression, President Colligan edited the language of the *Catalogue and Course of Study* to read: "Hunter College of the City of New York admits young women who wish to prepare themselves for many other professions (in addition to teaching) and avenues of service, each student choosing that in which she can best serve the City that educates her." He went on to explain that the new curriculum would fulfill two goals: to prepare the student to render service to the City of New York and to prepare her for life. While faculty and deans worked on practical curricular changes, the student body continued to ponder the threat of fascism. On November 29, 1938, the Student Council voted on a resolution proposed by the Zionist Avukah Club: "Student Council urges all students to boycott stores selling goods made in Germany, Austria, Sudeten Czechoslovakia, Japan and Italy." The resolution passed sixteen votes in favor with ten votes against.

Lillian Rosovsky (Ross), class of 1939, contributed to a long article in the January 1939 *Echo*, "The College Comments on Fascism." She noted that fascism was spreading throughout the world and that it was insidious and demagogic. Word manipulation, pious declarations of good intentions, public revelations of introspection, and clever maneuvers that are backed by ulterior motives are some characteristics of fascism that people ought to train themselves to recognize in case they should appear. She reminded her readers that fascism is opposed to all democratic ideals. She concluded: "Hunter College is preparing us to serve as citizens in a democracy. Therefore, any interference with or attempts to hinder student self-government by imposing arbitrary rules from above, is a tendency which serves reaction and pleases fascism."

Lillian was born in Syracuse, New York, to Edna and Louis Rosovsky, immigrants from Russia, on June 8, 1918. She began to be interested in journalism in junior high school when she was assigned an article in the school newspaper about a new school library. She was thrilled to see her writing in print. She wrote regularly for the *Echo* during her years at Hunter College. Her first job following graduation was at the left-leaning daily *PM*. From there she went to *The New Yorker*, where she remained for the rest of her career. She began writing "Talk of the Town" pieces and went on to become a staff writer. Her profile of Ernest Hemingway on a stopover in New York appeared in May 1950 and was a great success. She wrote a long article about John Huston's effort to make a film of Stephen Crane's *Red Badge of Courage*. The article was later reprinted as a book titled *Picture*. *Newsweek* called it the best book on Hollywood ever published. Among the hundreds of articles she wrote for the *New Yorker* were portraits of diamond merchant Harry Winston, fashion designer Coco Chanel, playwright Edward Albee, and film stars including Charlie Chaplin and Robin Williams. Late in life, in 1998, she wrote, *Here but Not Here: A Love Story*, about her fifty-year affair with William Shawn, the longtime editor of *The New Yorker*. Many colleagues accused her of betraying Shawn. The book appeared six years after Shawn's death. She was convinced that he would have liked being shown as he was. Lillian Ross died in 2017.

In June 1939, having won the battle over the future of the Park Avenue campus, President Colligan announced his intention to retire. Though he received public praise from the Board of Higher Education and from alumnae for leading the college in six different locations in Manhattan and in the new buildings in the Bronx, rumors that he had been forced into early retirement by the board circulated for years. During his tenure Student Council leaders like Bella Visono Dodd and Soia Mentschikoff, Music Club leader and conductor of the Hunter Symphony Orchestra Beatrice Brown, and *Echo* editor Lucy Schildkret Dawidowicz continued to exhibit the twin Hunter characteristics of excellence and activism. On September 8, the *Bulletin* announced the board's appointment of George Shuster as acting president and academic dean of Hunter College. Shuster had previously served in the English Departments of Notre Dame and St. Joseph's College for Women, and as editor of *Commonweal*. Shuster had served in World War I in intelligence; he was a prodigious writer—journalist, translator, and a writer of fiction and nonfiction. He would have a major influence on the continuing development of Hunter College.

Chapter Four

War and Peace (1939–1949)

The World's Fair in Flushing, Queens, whose theme was "The World of Tomorrow," opened in April 1939. Preparations for the fair at Hunter were directed by Professor Edna Wells Luetz, class of 1915, who led a team of faculty, students, and alumnae to document Hunter's effort to prepare young women to actively engage in the changing world. Next to displays of new technology including television, air conditioning, nylon stockings, and color film, Hunter provided musical entertainment, gymnastic exhibits, lectures, and a documentary film titled *Hunter Prepares Women for the World of Tomorrow*. The display, created for the Board of Higher Education by the four public colleges—Brooklyn, City, Hunter, and Queens—was prominently featured. Acting President George N. Shuster began his two-decade career at Hunter assisting Professor Luetz, faculty, and students in creating the display for the fair.

Several months later, on Hunter's seventieth birthday, February 14, 1940, Shuster was present to lay the cornerstone of the new sixteen-story modern building at 695 Park Avenue. Ordway Tead, chairman of the Board of Higher Education, expressed the feelings of many in the crowd: "We are here to seal the cornerstone of a habitation of shared learning, of associated truth-seeking, of organized and sustained inquiry into the ways of mankind's mastery of the world. . . . The College stands as . . . the great conservator of the spirit of truth-seeking."

The New York Times reported that invitations to attend the dedication of Hunter's new $6.5 million skyscraper and the inauguration of George N. Shuster as the fifth president of the college had been sent to eighteen hundred American colleges and universities, government officials, and organizations. The modern concrete, stone slab, and glass building, a contrast to the Gothic brick structure that it replaced, was scheduled to be ready for the opening day of classes on September 16. Shuster was installed on September 1, 1940. A full week of festivities marked the occasion and celebrated the simultaneous completion of the new building.

Poet Robert F. Tristram Coffin attended the ceremony and read a poem titled "The Palace of Park Avenue." Philosopher Jacques Maritain spoke about the need to create the type of culture that extols the moral element. Knowledge is not enough. "How to be," he said, is of greater importance than "how to do." Shuster concurred, explaining that the attributes of an educated person are freedom, progress, alertness, discipline, and courage. Despite the war raging in Europe, Shuster envisaged the immediate future as a time of promise of even wider perspectives, more broadly extended vistas of usefulness, and farther and broader horizons. He directed the architect to inscribe the inspiring words of Ralph Waldo Emerson on the north wall of the new building: "We are of different opinions at different hours, but we may always be said to be at heart on the side of truth."

Historian Lewis Mumford said the building was worthy of more praise than any college structure since Thomas Jefferson designed the University of Virginia. In an article in the *New Yorker*, he described the "Skyscraper School," with its well-equipped infirmary, several gymnasiums, a standard swimming pool, classrooms, offices, laboratories, and lounges. He lauded the library with space for one million books and reading rooms for a thousand students; art studios and music rooms as well as a playhouse were described. The student dining hall seated one thousand. Mumford found the Assembly Hall, seating three thousand, to be the finest thing of its kind in New York, in some respects better than Radio City Music Hall. The Associate Alumnae who had fought to rebuild on the Sixty-Eighth Street site presented the college with a new organ for the Assembly Hall.

On October 28, 1940, President Franklin Delano Roosevelt officiated at the ribbon-cutting ceremony for the Assembly Hall. Funding to complete the new building had been obtained from the Works Progress Administration, a New Deal program. A seventeen-year-old junior, Regina Resnik, a music major, a member of the Music Club and the Gilbert and Sullivan Society, was asked to sing the national anthem. She remembered the stage was decorated with flowers, the seal of the president of the United States, the flag of the City of New York, the American flag, and

Figure 4.1. Regina Resnik, 1942. *Source*: Archives and Special Collections, Hunter College Libraries, Hunter College of the City University of New York, New York City.

the Hunter College flag. President Roosevelt, aided by his sons, James and John, approached the lectern. The audience stood cheering. Resnik was announced, stood below the lectern, and sang the anthem. When she finished, she turned to the president and saw him mouth, "Thank you." Resnik, the daughter of immigrants, would go on to a career as an opera diva, singing all over the world, but she never forgot this moment.

Born in the Bronx in August 1922, Resnik began vocal training with famed soprano and voice coach Rosalie Miller at the age of thirteen and soon won $10 for appearing on the *Major Bowes Amateur Hour* on public radio. She turned down the offer of a scholarship to Julliard in favor of Hunter College, where she could also earn a teaching degree. Resnik graduated from Hunter in 1942 and debuted that year at the Brooklyn Academy of Music. In April 1944 she won the Metropolitan Opera Auditions of the Air and was awarded a contract with the company.

Later that year, substituting for Zinka Milanov, she was hailed for a stellar performance as Leonora in *Il Trovatore*, her debut with the Metropolitan Opera. A decade of performances as a soprano all over the world was followed by retraining her voice as a mezzo soprano and four decades of singing, directing, teaching, and acting.

Though Resnik was exceptionally talented, she was in many ways a typical Hunter alumna. Her best friend throughout her long life was Floria V. Lasky, a fellow student of immigrant background at Hunter. Lasky graduated first in her class at NYU Law School and had an outstanding career in entertainment law. Remembering their time at Hunter College, Lasky commented, "We took a sandwich in a little brown bag, and we took a quarter. Ten cents for carfare back and forth and five cents for a container of milk." Far from making immigrant girls feel ashamed of their poverty, Hunter College, she thought, made them feel capable. On the twenty-fifth anniversary of her Metropolitan Opera debut, Resnik established the Regina Resnik Scholarship Fund to provide awards to a new generation of talented and needy Hunter College students. In 1991, Resnik received the doctor of humane letters, *honoris causa*, from her alma mater. She died in 2013.

In his first annual report to the Board of Higher Education, President Shuster wrote: "A school which is primarily a cross-section of our society, which is recruited from all races, all classes, all faiths, ought under leadership which possesses a measure of integrity and intelligence to inculcate both self-reliance and mutual understanding." The *Wistarion* of 1940 included a description of student committees and clubs that exemplified Shuster's values. Among them were the Freshman Advisory Committee, which established Freshman Week; the Elections Committee, which supervised the elections of each class as well as elections for the Student Council; and the Board of Contract Review, which included the business managers of the three major student publications: *Bulletin*, *Echo*, and *Wistarion*. The Inter-Club Committee coordinated club events. There were several new clubs in 1940: Amateur Radio Club, American Student Union, Armenian Club, Caducean (pre-medical) Club, Karl Marx Club, and Youth Against War. The Pan-Hellenic Committee coordinated sorority events; and the House-Plan Association coordinated events for the House Plans, independent social groups that were not part of national sororities.

One of the remarkable students who graduated in January 1940 was Ivy Ophelia Roach (Brooks). Ivy was born in Brooklyn in 1916 to James and Mabel Roach, immigrants from Barbados. One aspect of her childhood was documented in the Black newspaper, *The New York Age*. Beginning in 1931, there were repeated references to the musical performances of young Ivy, who began as a member of the Junior Choir of Siloam Presbyterian Church, and later joined the orchestra of Grace M. Jones, performing as a violin soloist at the YMCA on Carlton Avenue. She also performed with the Gold Star Orchestra and Chorus, a unit of Atwell's Progressive Music League, where she served as president. Reports of her musical performances continued through February 1936.

Ivy attended Hunter College from 1936 to 1940. Presumably she studied physiology and nutrition, as she later took graduate work in these areas. Regrettably there is no information about her participation in school clubs or her academic achievements. Following graduation, Ivy became a member of the Epsilon chapter of the Zeta Phi Beta sorority, an organization with national membership that was founded at Howard University in 1920. The sorority encouraged high standards of scholastic achievement and commitment to addressing the ills and prejudices affecting humanity in general and the Black community in particular. Election of officers in February 1942 was held at her home, 158 Lefferts Place, Brooklyn.

Hitler invaded Poland while Ivy was a Hunter student. The US began an intense war preparedness program. The Army Nurse Corps expanded its recruiting process. Thousands of Black nurses filled out applications and received the following response: "Your application to the Army Nurse Corps cannot be given favorable consideration as there are no provisions in Army regulations for the appointment of colored nurses in the Corps." The National Association of Colored Graduate Nurses challenged this policy. In 1941, fifty-six Black nurses were belatedly admitted to the Army Nurse Corps. All were sent to segregated bases in the South. Roach was not among them. She was, however, a speaker at meetings called by the New York local of the National Association of Colored Graduate Nurses to secure interest in professional nurse training in New York hospitals. Despite a shortage of army nurses, by 1944, only three hundred Black women were accepted to serve in the Army Nurse Corps, compared to forty thousand white nurses. By the end of the war, the number of Black nurses in the military had grown to five hundred, out of fifty-nine thousand, and few had been sent overseas. Most cared for Black soldiers and prisoners of war in the United States.

Ivy Roach enrolled in Teachers College, Columbia, in fall 1942. She completed an internship at Harlem Hospital and was awarded an MS in nutrition in June 1944. Ivy joined the Women's Army Corps as a nurse and was given the rank of 2nd lieutenant. She was assigned to Camp Beale, California, a POW camp with a one-thousand-bed hospital. After the war, she taught nutrition to nursing students at Tuskegee Institute and participated in a research project about preeclampsia that was published in the *Journal of the National Medical Association* in 1949. In 1950, she used the GI Bill to attend Meharry Medical College, a historically Black medical school. Ivy Roach was one of five students accepted at Meharry from the Hunter graduating classes of 1940 to 1952. She graduated in 1954 and was hired as a radiologist at the Tuskegee VA (Veterans' Administration) Hospital. She moved to Tuskegee with her husband, Alfred D. Brooks, and had three children.

Dr. Roach spent several years at the VA Hospital in East Orange, New Jersey, learning how to use advanced radiological equipment. She was promoted to chief of radiology when she returned to Tuskegee in 1966 and served in that position for two decades. During this time, she also served as secretary of the National Medical Association, the Black counterpart to the segregated American Medical Association. At the Hunter centennial celebration in 1970, Ivy Roach Brooks was honored for her work in Tuskegee, and she was named Woman of the Year by Zeta Phi Beta, the sorority she had once hosted at her home in Brooklyn. Dr. Roach died in 1986.

Another student who had an interest in medicine and graduated in 1940 was Pearl Primus, born in Port of Spain, Trinidad, in 1919. Her mother's heritage was Ashanti from West Africa. Her father's family was German Jewish. When Pearl was two, she left Trinidad with her mother and brother, Edward, to join her father in New York City. By 1933, her excellent grades won her a place at Hunter College High School. She graduated in 1937 and continued her studies at Hunter College. Pearl, who majored in biology, started to train for dance in her sophomore year at the New Dance Group, an integrated, progressive dance collective. Professor Elsie V. Steedman of the Anthropology Department encouraged her to develop her talents as a dancer. In her senior year, the multitalented Primus submitted a poem to the *Echo.* "Song," which is based on the Trinidadian dialect of her childhood, was published in April 1940. It was the first piece in the literary magazine to be published in nonstandard English:

> You know how the sky looks wen it's goin' a rain . . .
> Jes sullen an' sad an' kind plain . . .
> Lik' the heavens ain't ever goin' smile again . . .
> You know . . .

You know how 'tis wen the rain' gins ta fall
On the roofs an' the sidewalks—in the gutters an all . . .
Lik' the angels ain't goin' stop cryin' at all . . .
You know . . .
An den wen the warm earth agins to dry . . .
An the sun's face's a grinnin' up there in the sky
I clutch to my heart les it jump up an'fly . . .
You know . . .

After graduation Primus worked a variety of war-related jobs. She was a welder, a clerk, a switchboard operator, a teacher, and an athlete, all the while continuing to study dance.

On February 14, 1943, Primus had her professional premiere at the Ninety-Second Street Y. Her performance included "A Man Has Just Been Lynched," set to the song "Strange Fruit," which was made popular by Billie Holiday; "Greetings from South America," using Brazilian music; "African Ceremonial," with the music from "Conga Kongo." Her career received another boost in May 1943 when she had a two-week engagement at Café Society Downtown, an integrated nightclub. She also performed at the Stage Door Canteen and the Music Box Canteen, nightclubs for members of the armed forces. On June 7 she performed at the first Negro Freedom Rally at Madison Square Garden, which included Paul Robeson, Canada Lee, and Duke Ellington.

In 1946, Primus took graduate classes in education at Teachers College and continued to perform with a company she founded. Three years later, she traveled to Africa on a grant from the Julius Rosenwald Foundation. She lived with tribes in Nigeria and the Belgian Congo, observing and recording African dances, ceremonies, and cultural activities. She performed for King George VI and Queen Mary in 1951 in London and at the inauguration of Liberian president William V. S. Tubman in 1952. She married Percival Borde, a choreographer and dancer she met in Trinidad, in 1954. The couple performed together until Borde's death in 1979.

In 1963, following a second long trip to Africa funded by the Rebecca Harkness Foundation, Primus founded the Primus-Borde School of Dance, where she developed methods of cross-cultural education through dance. She explained: "I dance not to entertain but to help people better understand each other. Because through dance I have experienced the wordless joy of freedom. I seek it more fully now for my people and for *all* people everywhere."

In 1969, while pursuing a doctorate in anthropology at NYU, Primus was appointed a professor at Hunter. She later taught at several colleges, including Howard and NYU. She received many awards, including a Star of Africa decoration from the Liberian government and the Scroll of Honor from the National Council of Negro Women. In 1991, she was awarded the National Medal of Arts by President George H. W. Bush, the first Hunter alumna to be so honored. Primus died in 1994.

In 1941, a year after the graduation of Ivy Roach and Pearl Primus, Rosalyn Sussman (Yalow) and Ada Louise Landman (Huxtable) joined the ranks of Hunter alumnae. Each made significant contributions, one in physics and medicine, and the other in architectural criticism. Rosalyn Sussman was born in 1921 in New York City. Her mother was a German Jewish immigrant; her father was born on the Lower East Side. Neither parent had a high school education. There were no books in their house, but Rosalyn went to the public library every week and took home four or five books.

By the seventh grade, Rosalyn was committed to mathematics. In high school, a great chemistry teacher inspired her interest. At Hunter College, her interests were diverted to physics by Professor Herbert N. Otis. In 1937, she was thrilled by Eve Curie's biography of her mother, Marie Curie. In January 1939, she attended a lecture at Columbia given by Enrico Fermi on the new discovery of nuclear fission. Though her parents thought she should become an elementary school teacher, Rosalyn persisted and became the first student to graduate as a physics major at Hunter College.

Six months later, she received the offer of a teaching assistantship in physics at the University of Illinois. At the first meeting of the faculty of the College of Engineering she discovered that she was the only woman among its four hundred members. The dean told her that she was the first woman on the faculty since 1917. The attack on Pearl Harbor had led to the mobilization of many faculty to secret scientific work elsewhere. Young Army and Navy recruits were a new presence on the campus. In 1943, Rosalyn married Aaron Yalow, a fellow physics graduate student. Her life was busy with a heavy teaching load, graduate courses, a thesis requiring long hours in the laboratory, and wartime housekeeping with its shortages and rationing.

Rosalyn Yalow received her PhD in nuclear physics in January 1945. She returned to New York City and a position as an assistant engineer at the Federal Communications Laboratory, a research lab for International

Telephone and Telegraph. She was the only woman engineer on the staff. When her research group left New York City in 1946, Yalow returned to Hunter College to teach physics. Most of her students on the Bronx campus were returning veterans (see the "Legacy of Hunter College" chapter about the admissions of veterans to the Bronx campus).

In December 1947, Yalow was hired by the Bronx Veterans Administration (VA) as a part-time consultant, continuing to teach at Hunter until spring semester 1950. At that time, she left teaching and joined the VA full time. Several months later, Dr. Solomon A. Berson joined her lab at the VA. They worked together for twenty-two years until his death in 1972. Their research led to the ability to measure plasma insulin in humans. Many more years of work in the laboratory led to a further application of this measurement, the development of the radioimmunoassay. This technique led to advances in the field of endocrinology, making possible changes in diabetes research and in diagnosing and treating hormonal problems. Yalow won the Nobel Prize in Physiology or Medicine in 1977 for their joint work. She was the first Hunter alumna to be so honored.

Reflecting on her experiences as a scientist in her Nobel Prize acceptance speech, Yalow explained that new ideas are not accepted immediately. It took three years from the time of Yalow and Berson's discovery until the process was made practical and an additional five years for the scientific community to adopt the new process. Yalow also commented on the discrimination she experienced as a woman scientist. She believed that the fundamental problem was that people who are discriminated against begin to think of themselves as second class. This belief keeps them from succeeding. In contrast, Yalow knew that there was something wrong with the discrimination, not something wrong with her.

In 1976 Yalow found time to manage and host a five-part dramatic series on the life of Madame Curie for the Public Broadcasting Service. She continued to do research at the VA and received numerous awards and honorary degrees. She died in 2011.

Ada Louise Landman (Huxtable) was born in 1921. She grew up an only child in a comfortable, middle-class Jewish family living in Manhattan in a Beaux-Arts apartment house on Central Park West and Eighty-Ninth Street. She was familiar with the Metropolitan Museum of Art, the American Museum of Natural History, and Central Park. Her father, a physician and playwright, died when she was eleven. Her mother was not supportive of college education for girls, but Ada Louise wanted to go to college. Since the family had no money, the only possibility was Hunter College.

At Hunter she majored in art, became president of the Art Club, worked on the *Freshman Handbook*, served on the Dean's Committee, was on the *Wistarion* staff, performed in Varsity, and was elected to Phi Beta Kappa.

Following in the footsteps of Professor Edna Wells Luetz, Ada Louise worked on set designs for Hunter productions. She was praised in *The New York Times* for her designs for *The Yellow Jacket* in 1940 and *H.M.S. Pinafore* in 1941. Ada Louise entered an interior decorating contest at Bloomingdale's with a friend. They won the $100 prize, a lot of money for the students. Following graduation in 1941, unable to find a job, she wrote to the president of Bloomingdale's explaining that she had won the contest and needed a job. The president interviewed and hired her.

She worked in the furniture department, which was preparing to sell items selected in the Museum of Modern Art design competition. Ada Louise married L. Garth Huxtable, an industrial designer who came in to buy furniture. She received a fellowship for graduate study in architectural history at the Institute of Fine Arts at NYU and studied there part-time from 1942 to 1950. To the surprise of her professors, Ada Louise Huxtable wrote papers about the first public housing in NYC, not about Baroque churches.

From 1946 to 1950 she served as curatorial assistant for architecture and design at the Museum of Modern Art. She was hired by Philip Johnson and worked with him on the Mies van der Rohe show at the museum in 1947. In 1950 she received a Fulbright Scholarship that enabled her to spend a year traveling in Italy studying Italian architecture and engineering. She brought back a large photographic file of early twentieth-century architectural styles. She started writing art criticism for *Art News* and *Progressive Architecture.* In 1958 she received a Guggenheim Fellowship to study progressive architecture in the United States.

In 1963, Ada Louise Huxtable was named the first architectural critic at *The New York Times*. She held that position until 1982. Her daily column made architecture an important aspect of public dialogue. She spoke out against projects lacking civic engagement. She was the second woman to win a Pulitzer Prize for the *Times* when she was awarded the first prize given for distinguished criticism in 1970. Three years later she was named a member of the editorial board of the *Times.* Her book, *Will They Ever Finish Bruckner Boulevard?*, was well received. In 1974, she was elected a fellow of the American Academy of Arts and Sciences. She was appointed a MacArthur Fellow in 1981, and in 1989, she became a member of the American Philosophical Society. In 1997 she was named architecture critic for *The Wall Street Journal.* She held that position until her death in January 2013. Huxtable wrote ten books on architecture, including a biography of Frank Lloyd Wright.

While Yalow and Huxtable achieved professional success in New York City, Marjorie Henderson (Ellis), who also graduated in 1941, went to California to buy land and establish a career. Marjorie was born in 1915 in Seabrook, South Carolina, on a farm belonging to her grandfather, Toby Jacob Scriven, who had been a slave for the first twelve years of his life. Scriven worked hard, saved money, bought land, and pursued opportunities for education. Seabrook was a small town of several hundred farmers who grew cotton, corn, sugar cane, and assorted vegetables. Marjorie's mother, Lily, was not married. She left her daughter on her father's farm where she was brought up by her aunts, Jenny and May, and her uncle, Jake. As a young child, Marjorie suffered painful burns and scarring when she fell into an outdoor fire set for boiling clothes. The recovery was long and painful as her only treatment was rest and she was left with many scars.

Marjorie went to a one-room schoolhouse, the first Black elementary school in the area, built on land donated by her grandfather. She excelled at school, as was expected of a "Scriven." Though some white neighbors called the school the "Toby Scriven School for Niggers," Marjorie remembered it as very pleasant place. Students sat on long wooden benches and wrote on slates with chalk; they didn't do much writing; they recited their lessons orally. The teacher, a Black woman who had been educated "up North," taught the children "Lift Every Voice and Sing," the Black national anthem, and told them about George Washington Carver, the Black agricultural scientist. There were no discipline problems in the school; those who misbehaved were expelled. There were recesses and picnics, spelling bees, and other competitions.

In 1927, when Marjorie was eleven, her grandfather died. Marjorie was sent to live with Lily in Philadelphia. There she began to care for four younger half-siblings while her mother worked. In 1932, her mother, recently widowed, moved the family to Harlem hoping to earn enough money to raise her children. Lily did piecework as a power sewing machine operator. Marjorie cooked and looked after the younger children. She continued to excel in school, skipping grades. Marjorie also encountered Northern-style racism; she was shown the back entrance of the auditorium for the awards ceremony when she won a school debating competition. She felt that whites treated Blacks like that regularly. It "burned you up inside." Nevertheless, she persisted in learning from teachers who encouraged her to go to the library. She had very few books at home as her mother had had very little education. She followed the advice of her teachers, Black and white, about nutrition, making sure she fed her siblings vegetables as her teachers recommended. In high school she loved the Russian novels that she borrowed from the library. She became interested in science and assumed she would go to college and teach science. Marjorie became a Girl Scout. Membership in her troop was limited to Black girls; they met in a church basement. They did arts and crafts, nature study, day trips, occasionally overnighters outdoors. The Scouts emphasized community service; the girls made gifts for people in homes for the aged and hospitals, also for children in orphanages.

Marjorie's scars were the source of teasing when she was in junior high school. She was called "scarface," the title of a popular movie of the time. Her friends were neighborhood children who were mostly Black. Marjorie enrolled at Hunter College in 1935, majoring in biological sciences. Most of her friends there were white, but she held back, not taking her acquaintances into her confidence because "there are certain things you don't divulge to the enemy." It took her six years to graduate because she was forced to find paid work to support herself. Marjorie was awarded a National Youth Administration job that paid $22 per month. She also worked in private homes to earn money. She frequently wondered if all her efforts were worthwhile, as she was aware that racism denied her uncles, who were college graduates, appropriate employment. Her aunt, Pearl, taught in a rural school in winter and came north in summer to do menial work in private homes to supplement her meager income. Marjorie was encouraged to believe that she could succeed despite the experiences of her relatives by holding fast to the words of the preamble of the Constitution: "All men are created equal." She was fortified by the "Ain't I a Woman?" speech of Sojourner Truth. Like Rosalyn Yalow, Marjorie understood that there was something wrong with discrimination, not something wrong with her. She reflected, "I just know that I was as good as anybody created."

At Hunter, Marjorie founded the Phyllis Wheatley Negro Study Club, named for the first published African American poet and supporter of the American Revolution. Membership grew to fifteen students who did research and reports on African American contributions to life and culture. Sometimes club members put on short programs. One of the members, Pearl Primus, would later incorporate African traditions in her dance performances. Marjorie, like Pearl, was a biology major; she minored in natural science, taking classes in physics, chemistry, anthropology, and geology. Her graduating class in 1941 included eight hundred students. First Lady Eleanor Roosevelt was their commencement speaker.

Following graduation, Marjorie Henderson headed west to California with her Hunter BA, determined to get a teaching job and to buy some land. She traveled cross country by train and went to live with an aunt and later at the YWCA. She expected to take graduate courses at UCLA to obtain a California teaching license, but she was rebuffed by an admissions clerk who informed her that no one would hire a Black teacher. As a result, Marjorie decided to get a job in the war industry. In the hiring process she again experienced discrimination, but she was persistent and ultimately was hired to work on an assembly line by North American Aviation. Marjorie reported that she was devastated by the discrimination she experienced. She began to fear she had wasted six years getting her degree. Nevertheless, she saved her money and bought three acres of land.

In 1947 she met and married Russell Ellis, who had a teenage son. Ellis had attended college, played professional baseball for the Negro league, and served in the army, where he was among the soldiers who landed on Normandy Beach on D-Day. Ellis returned from battle wounded and weary. The Ellis family bought a house in Carver Manor Annex, in South Los Angeles, a middle-class Black neighborhood. Russell Ellis had studied architecture but was unable to get a job in his field. He worked for decades as a clerk in the post office. Marjorie was hired by the Los Angeles Unified School District to teach third grade at the 102nd Street School in Watts. She taught there for thirty-four years. She also enrolled at California State University, Los Angeles, where she took graduate courses in school administration and teaching reading and was awarded an MA.

Though she was qualified to be a school administrator, she never sought a job in that area as she didn't want to face discrimination again. Marjorie concluded: "There's so much energy that's wasted in being Black. While the average white person just has to be qualified, we've got to be qualified plus. And then pray that they will accept us. That is extremely unfair." She reflected on the years that passed following her Hunter degree and her first teaching job in Los Angeles. The reason for the delay was the fact that she was Black. There was no policy against hiring Black teachers, but the schools found all sorts of reasons not to hire them.

Once she got into the classroom to teach, Marjorie faced a new challenge: pupils who were not motivated to learn. Parents who had migrated from the South and were struggling to put food on the table had little time to devote to encouraging their children to learn. That responsibility was given to the teachers. Marjorie had planned to teach high school biology, but there were few high school jobs available and many elementary school positions open. She used the science education she had received at Hunter to become a science specialist in her elementary school. She tried to communicate her love of learning to her pupils. She also tried to impress upon her students the dignity of working. She wanted them to give back to the community, not to only be consumers. Ultimately, her pupils taught her to be more tolerant, more patient. She learned to fit her teaching to the individual pupil, as children learn in different ways. She was delighted when one of her pupils, Stan Saunders, became a Rhodes Scholar.

Like Ivy Roach, Marjorie joined Zeta Phi Beta, a national Black sorority. Her chapter, Alpha Psi Zeta, supported education in Honduras and was active in voter registration in Los Angeles. She was also a volunteer tutor to the Girls' Club of LA and an instructor for the AARP Mature Safe Driving Program for seniors. She was a member of Black Educators and the chairman of the Oratorical Contest Committee for Negro History Week. She argued that educators must make education relevant to the lives of their pupils while parents must reinforce education at home. She urged her fellow teachers to incorporate more information about Black history in the elementary school curriculum.

In 1967, Marjorie was selected by the US Agency for International Development to participate in its first international Teach Corps. She was one of six American teachers sent to teach methodology to teachers in Kathmandu, Nepal. Each of them was assigned to work at a specific grade level. Marjorie worked with third grade teachers. She maintained a connection with the teachers she worked with in Nepal for many years. In 1969, she was recognized by Zeta Phi Beta as Woman of the Year for her community service and for her work in Nepal. Marjorie retired in 1981. She joined the National Association of University Women, the Black counterpart to the American Association of University Women, which encouraged Black students to attend college. She died in 2022.

The semester after Marjorie Henderson Ellis graduated, Bella Savitsky (Abzug) was elected president of the Student Council, the leader of four thousand girls. Bella was born in 1920 to Russian immigrants in the Bronx. Her father, who owned the Live and Let Live Meat Market, died when Bella was thirteen. Her mother immediately went to work to support the family. Despite the hardships of the Depression, Bella recalled that her parents believed deeply in the promise of America and taught her to be responsible for taking charge of her life and for contributing to society. She also remembered that boys and girls were treated differently. Bella wanted a bicycle, but her parents said that bicycle riding wasn't safe for girls. She liked playing marbles in the street with boys. Again, her parents were opposed. On the other hand, when she asked to have Hebrew lessons, something often reserved for Jewish boys in her era, her father agreed to pay for the lessons. Bella credited her mother for building her confidence. She encouraged Bella and her sister to excel in their studies.

At Hunter, Bella majored in political science, was president of her freshman and junior classes, president of the Political Science Club, and president of the Student Council in 1940–1941. Determined to devote herself to social justice in America, she participated in peace strikes and

Figure 4.2. Bella Savitsky (Abzug), Student Council president, 1941. *Source*: Archives and Special Collections, Hunter College Libraries, Hunter College of the City University of New York, New York City.

decided to become a lawyer. Following graduation from Hunter in 1942, she applied to Harvard Law School, having heard that it was the best law school in the US. She received a letter, like the one received by Pauli Murray, that the law school did not accept women. Bella's mother told her to apply to Columbia where she would probably get a scholarship, and she could live at home and ride the subway for a nickel.

Bella followed two remarkable Hunter graduates to Columbia Law School. Ida Klaus, Hunter class of 1927, was one of three women in the first class to admit women at Columbia Law. She was invited to Washington by one of her professors, Herman Oliphant, who went to work for President Roosevelt in 1933. She was soon hired by the new National Labor Relations Board. She remained in Washington until 1954 when she was hired as counsel to Mayor Robert F. Wagner's new Department of Labor in New York City. In 1962 she was appointed to the position of director of staff relations for the New York City Board of Education. Nancy Fraenkel Wechsler, Hunter class of 1937, graduated from Columbia Law School in 1940. She earned the James Kent Scholarship in recognition of her academic achievement. She also won the Ordronaux Prize, awarded to the student achieving the highest academic average in each graduating class. By 1946, she was hired as counsel to President Harry Truman's Committee on Civil Rights. She joined Greenbaum, Wolf & Ernst in 1948, gaining attention because the firm represented Planned Parenthood at a time when contraception and abortion were illegal. In 1973, she was the author of an amicus brief for *Roe v. Wade*.

At Columbia, Bella was interested in labor law. In her second year of studies, she was selected for Law Review and married Martin Abzug, a young businessman, novelist, and World War II veteran. Martin typed her final papers. Bella graduated at the top of her class in 1944. Despite her academic success, when Bella applied for jobs, she was asked if she could type. She couldn't and decided not to learn. For decades she defended workers and was angered by the discourteous behavior of male union leaders and judges. She also defended Hollywood actors who were accused of being communists during the McCarthy witch hunts of the early 1950s. She took on the case of Willie McGee, a Black Mississippian sentenced to death on the charge of raping a white woman with whom he had a long consensual union. Bella traveled to the South where she slept in a bus station when no hotel would provide McGee's lawyer with a room. Despite her efforts, McGee was executed.

In 1961, Bella, who had participated in peace strikes while she was a Hunter student, helped organize Women Strike for Peace, leading thousands of women, mothers, and youngsters on lobbying expeditions to Congress and the White House on behalf of a ban on nuclear weapons testing. At the age of fifty, she decided to run for Congress on a women's rights and peace platform. Her campaign slogan was "This woman's place is in the House—the House of Representatives." She was the first Jewish woman to be elected to Congress, but not the first Hunter graduate. Edna Flannery Kelly had been elected in 1949. After taking her oath of office in 1971, Bella was sworn in again on the Capitol steps by Representative Shirley Chisholm, promising to "work for new priorities to heal the domestic wounds of war and use our country's wealth for life, not death." Her first official act was to introduce a resolution calling on President Nixon to withdraw all US forces from Vietnam. She advocated passage of the Equal Rights Amendment, wrote the first law banning discrimination against women seeking credit, and introduced legislation calling for comprehensive child care, Social Security for homemakers, and abortion rights.

Following three terms in Congress, Bella held leading positions in several national and international efforts to improve conditions for women. Like Eleanor Roosevelt, with whom she once shared a stage at Hunter, Bella saw a connection between sexism, racism, poverty, and institutional violence. Like Hillary Clinton, she saw women's rights as human rights. Her last efforts to make the world a better place were devoted to environmental issues. A lecture series in her name was started by the Women's Studies program at Hunter in the early 1980s. Bella remained close to many of her Hunter friends throughout her life. She died in 1998.

The last months of Bella Savitsky's term as president of Student Council coincided with American entry into World War II. The *Wistarion* captured the feelings of Bella's classmates:

> Soon we recognized the demands which a nation at war for its life must make on its women. December 7 placed many of us on the rostra of the civilian defense authorities. We were acting as air raid wardens. We were knitting for our menfolk in the services. We had registered for courses in defense. Many of us were preparing to enter the service of our government in administrative and personnel work, and all were ready to shoulder the jobs left unfilled by our country's fighters.

The new Hunter College building, which was the only fireproof structure in the neighborhood, became the center of emergency drills following the attack on Pearl Harbor in December 1941. President Shuster chaired a defense committee of faculty trained to prepare for an air attack. Assistance for the war effort was widespread among faculty, students, and alumnae. Ambulances were bought; blood was donated. Wartime activities for servicemen were again organized by alumnae under the leadership of Elizabeth Kallman, class of 1902, who reinstituted the Patriotic Service Committee created during World War I. The Hunter Canteen at the Hotel Woodward became a gathering place for armed service personnel on leave in New York City. Committee members volunteered to visit hospitals serving wounded veterans.

The War Service Training Program at Hunter was adopted after weeks of review of military needs by a committee organized by President

Figure 4.3. The War Committee: Shirley Braun, Kayleen Nagle, Gloria Agrin (chairman, spring semester), Alice Levine (chairman, fall semester), Minnie Riback, Aline Kaplan, Thelma Gilman, Ann Kraus, 1943. *Source*: Archives and Special Collections, Hunter College Libraries, Hunter College of the City University of New York, New York City.

Shuster. Students majoring in chemistry, physics, and statistics could take designated classes that were part of their major field. Students majoring in English might decide to take war service training in meteorology, or an art major might take a minor in chemistry. Others trained to become draftsmen for the armed services and for industry. Still others were trained as translators of foreign languages for government agencies and industry, as blueprint readers, and economic analysts. Hunter was the first civilian school in the nation to offer courses in cryptography and cryptanalytics. Other classes taught maps and map interpretation, military German, military French, and American naval history. During the war, more than forty special courses were added to the Hunter curriculum including nursing classes to meet a shortage caused by the war.

Recent graduates who majored in Romance languages were hired as French, Italian, and Spanish censors, and as broadcast monitors for the Foreign Broadcast Intelligence Division of the Federal Communications Commission. English and pre-journalism majors were employed by the Office of War Information, radio broadcasting companies, national news agencies, and a variety of newspapers. Political science graduates worked as teachers, policewomen, and law clerks, and did personnel work in war industries. Math department graduates did statistical research for the Federal Reserve Bank and ballistics statistics for the US Navy. Chemistry majors worked in industry and hospitals. Geology majors provided support to the Army Map Service. Physics majors were hired as research assistants in war plants and in special war projects in universities.

In the summer of 1942, four women's colleges, Wellesley, Smith, Bryn Mawr, and Hunter, participated in an Office of Education program offering training in radio technology, drafting, physics, and basic engineering. Other Hunter students spent months working on farms in upstate New York. This work was directed by the "Farm for Freedom" program. Hunter students donated blood to the Red Cross, served as air wardens, bought war stamps and bonds, and collected books for the armed forces. The college agreed to vacate the Bronx campus to serve as a training ground for Women Accepted for Volunteer Emergency Service (WAVES), a branch of the Naval Reserves. Thousands of students were crowded into the Park Avenue campus, giving the Bronx campus to thousands of women recruits.

Eugenie Clark, known as Genie, graduated during the war and went on to remarkable achievements despite experiencing anti-Japanese racism. Genie was born in 1922 and grew up in New York City. Her mother was Japanese; her father was an American who disappeared when Genie was a baby. From early childhood Genie was a devoted visitor to the New York Aquarium. She was fascinated by fish. She had a favorite elementary school teacher who took excellent students on field trips. She encouraged them to pick up whatever they found—snakes, insects, plants, weeds—for study. The teacher told Genie's mother that her daughter would probably be a scientist. In fourth grade Genie met Norma Denman (Woodburn). The girls remained friends for the rest of their lives. Genie's report card was all A's except for deportment where she sometimes got an F for fighting with boys who teased her about being Japanese. After graduating from P.S. 76, Genie and Norma enrolled at William Cullen Bryant High School in Queens. She was the only student of Japanese descent in the school. Genie, though small, was an enthusiastic basketball player in high school. Both girls graduated in 1939, and both passed the entrance exam for Hunter, which had become known as a "brainy" girls' school. Since more students applied than could be accepted, the grade point average (GPA) required for admission climbed to 97.5 percent at this time.

Students who failed to maintain a high GPA at Hunter were expelled. In her first semester at Hunter, Genie received A's in biology and math, a D in chemistry, and F's in English and German. Her GPA was below the minimum required to remain at Hunter. Dean Mary M. Fay called her in for a meeting seeking to understand the extreme discrepancy in her grades. The dean reported that Genie's English teacher said she was "hopeless" and that she flunked chemistry and German, but that her math and biology teachers said she was the best in the class and an exceptionally good student. Dean Fay asked Genie why she thought she got those grades. As she spoke, she noticed that Genie had fallen asleep. Dean Fay took Genie to the school nurse who said that she was so anemic she should have been in a hospital.

Based on the diagnosis and on Professor Mina Rees's recommendation, Genie was allowed to continue at Hunter. She still fell asleep in her chemistry class, but her English teacher was impressed with her interesting compositions, although she wondered why every story was about fish. Her compositions that semester formed the beginning of her best-selling autobiography, *Lady with a Spear*. She dedicated the book "to Professor Frederika Beatty who made a freshman course in composition as fascinating as one in ichthyology."

At the end of her sophomore year, Genie's biology teacher, Professor Theodora Nelson, recommended that she attend a summer course at the

University of Michigan Biological Station located on the south shore of Douglas Lake in the woods of northern Michigan; the station was one of the oldest and largest inland biological stations in the nation. Genie and her childhood friend, Norma, succeeded in raising the money to attend classes on field zoology and botany at the biological station, which was known as "Bug Camp." The faculty were all distinguished. Professor Charles W. Creaser taught ichthyology and herpetology. Genie and Norma, who had never been away from home, spent two summers at the camp and returned determined to become biologists.

After Pearl Harbor, Genie experienced some hostility from Hunter students. She recalled that she had endured a lot worse in elementary school. Genie graduated in September 1942 with a BA in zoology, botany, and chemistry. Jobs for biologists were almost nonexistent. There were want ads for entry level positions for chemistry, physics, and math majors. Genie was hired by Celanese Corporation in Newark; her friend Norma soon found a job there too. Genie and Norma also began to take graduate classes at NYU.

Genie studied with Charles M. Breder Jr., who became her mentor and had a major influence on her professional life as a scientist. His ichthyology course was held at the American Museum of Natural History. Breder encouraged her to present a paper at the American Society of Ichthyologists and Herpetologists in 1946. Genie was offended by anti-Japanese sentiment in the group, but relieved when a vote to bar those of Japanese heritage was narrowly defeated. In response to Genie's paper, Professor Carl Hubbs of the Scripps Institution of Oceanography at the University of California at San Diego offered her a job as his assistant and a place in the PhD program. She shared a ride to San Diego and began working with Hubbs who introduced her to diving with a mask and helmet so that she could begin to observe the life of fish.

Genie returned to New York in 1948, invited to work with Myron Gordon, a geneticist working at the New York Aquarium and the American Museum of Natural History. He offered to sponsor her doctoral work at NYU. At this time the field of ichthyology was limited to naming and cataloging fishes. The goal was to collect specimens of new species and describe them. Even with the development of scuba gear, studying fish behavior and life history remained difficult because divers could only stay underwater for an hour. Genie mastered diving techniques that allowed her to stay underwater long enough to study the life of fish. She earned her doctorate in 1950 and spent the decade doing research in Micronesia under a grant from the Office of Naval Research and in the Red Sea under a Fulbright Scholarship, while raising four children.

When Genie presented her research about the Red Sea fish in Florida, Anne and William Vanderbilt were in the audience. In 1955 they built her a lab, the Cape Haze Marine Laboratory, to continue her work in the Florida Keys. Genie conducted behavioral, reproductive, and anatomical experiments on sharks and other fish. In 1968 she accepted a position at the University of Maryland, retiring in 1999. She returned to her laboratory in Florida, now renamed the Mote Marine Laboratory, in 2000 and remained an active researcher and diver until her death in 2015. She received many awards and honors, including from the US Postal Service, which honored her with a Forever stamp featuring a shark and Genie in diving gear.

About the time of Genie's graduation from Hunter, the double townhouse on Sixty-Fifth Street that had been home to Sara Delano Roosevelt (Franklin's mother) and to Eleanor and Franklin Roosevelt was put on the market. A nonprofit consortium organized by President Shuster purchased the house to be used by Hunter students to foster interreligious and interracial cooperation. The dedication ceremony held in November 1943 was attended by Eleanor Roosevelt who remained actively involved with Hunter students for the rest of her life. The issues of antisemitism and racism that were heightened by the war raised the awareness of those sharing the house.

Klara Apat (Silverstein) frequented the Hillel Club at Roosevelt House. She became friends with students attending meetings of the Toussaint L'Ouverture Club since they had adjoining meeting rooms. Helene D. Goldfarb was a member of Alpha Omega Pi, the interracial nonsectarian sorority, which also held meetings at Roosevelt House. She went there two or three times a week during her four years at Hunter. She remembered walking down Park Avenue from the college to Roosevelt House with Ruby Saunders, her Black friend. Passersby stared at the two women, because their friendship was out of the ordinary. Yet, Helene emphasized, at Hunter and at Roosevelt House it was perfectly ordinary.

A few months before the dedication of Roosevelt House, an article in *The New York Times* announced the creation of a new club, the Wistarians (not to be confused with *Wistarion*, the college yearbook), a group of 150 Black Hunter alumnae who adopted a program designed to promote better understanding among racial groups. The group protested the Navy's presence on the Bronx campus since the Navy barred Black women from enlisting. Their goal was "to open up that closed door."

In February 1943, the American Negro Culture course was added to the college curriculum, following years of pressure from the Toussaint L'Ouverture Club. The course described the origins of Black people, the organization of African society, interaction between Africa, Europe, and the New World, the institution of slavery in the United States, the social status of Blacks, and their cultural contributions. In connection with the course, a shelf of books dealing with Black culture was added to the library. The Wistarians hosted a reception for Professor Adelaide Cromwell Hill, a part-time faculty member, who was hired to teach the course. Hill was a Smith College graduate, with a master of social work degree from Bryn Mawr, and a PhD in sociology from Radcliffe. She was the first part-time Black faculty member at Hunter College. In 1946, Professor Mary Huff Diggs, a Phi Beta Kappa graduate with degrees from Bryn Mawr, the University of Minnesota, Fisk University, and the University of Pennsylvania, was hired by the Sociology Department, the first Black full-time tenure-track professor. Not long thereafter, Professor Lawanda Cox, a second Black full-time faculty member, was hired by the History Department. Cox was a pioneer in the study of racism in the Jim Crow South.

The Toussaint L'Ouverture Club, established in 1937, continued to develop in this period. In 1942, Frances Benson, Elaine Bailey, Marjorie Mullet, and Sylvia Alves represented the club at the National Congress of Negro Youth meeting held in Washington, DC. In October 1943, three delegates were sent to the meeting of the youth group of the National Association for the Advancement of Colored People held at Lincoln University in Pennsylvania. The Toussaint L'Ouverture Club organized an anti-poll tax meeting at the college; eight student clubs, differing widely in political beliefs, united behind the common goal of protesting poll taxes. One thousand postcards were sent to senators, and funds were collected to send telegrams as an outcome of the meeting. Toussaint members also volunteered to work as big sisters at the Riverdale Orphanage Asylum, which housed two hundred Black children from eight to sixteen years old. Members visited the children, wrote letters, took them on trips, and invited them to their homes. The members also volunteered at the Harlem Defense Recreation Center during the war.

Another student who graduated during the war, Ruby Ann Wallace (Dee), was born in 1922 in Cleveland, Ohio, but soon moved to Harlem. She was raised by her father, Edward Nathaniel Wallace, a waiter and cook on railroads, and her stepmother, Emma Amelia Benson, who had attended Atlanta University and studied with W. E. B. DuBois. Despite financial difficulties, Ruby was given piano, violin, and dancing lessons. She also observed neighbors being evicted from their homes and knew that her family was nearly evicted too.

At P.S. 136, Ruby was an excellent student, but the school did not encourage students to take the tests for competitive high schools like Hunter College High School (HCHS). Ruby's stepmother led a group of parents to demand a change in the policy. As a result, nine students were selected to take the test. After taking a practice exam, the math teacher realized that her students needed more training. The nine stayed after school for three days a week to study math. All nine passed the test with high marks.

In the fall of 1936, Ruby started at HCHS. Her grades were good enough for her to enroll, but she faced a new and challenging environment. Her classmates seemed so sure of themselves; they were well dressed, spoke casually of family vacations, and were smart. At HCHS, she benefited from art classes that taught her to draw and paint. She was found to be nearsighted and was fitted for glasses. Her Hunter experiences were in sharp contrast to the lessons she learned in her neighborhood where she observed that men routinely cheated on their wives and beat them. Ruby's parents had divorced after violence at home. She also heard criticism of HCHS. One of her male friends explained that fellas didn't want to hang out with her because she was a Hunter girl. Hunter girls had a bad reputation. They were considered too smart, not attractive to boys. Ruby struggled with the differences between her neighborhood values and those she learned at HCHS. Overcoming these challenges, Ruby graduated from HCHS in June 1939 and entered Hunter College in September.

Ruby wanted to be an actor; she enrolled in French and Spanish classes as well as classes in Chinese and Portuguese. She also took stenography, thinking she might become a court reporter. During her second semester at Hunter, Abram Hill and Fred O'Neal started the American Negro Theatre in the basement of the public library on 135th Street. Ruby auditioned for the part of Cobina in Hill's *On Strivers Row.* She won the part. She also continued to take dance classes and piano lessons and belonged to the Interracial Baptist Youth Fellowship where she created artwork. With all the extracurricular work, it's not surprising that she received a letter from the dean at the end of her first year: "We regret to inform you that your grades have fallen below the requirements to remain a matriculated student in the day program." Ruby registered for summer school and night school. She took the necessary remedial classes and was reinstated at the end of the following year. Ruby graduated with a major in Romance languages in 1944 at the end of five years.

In her memoir, Ruby credited the literature classes she took for giving her a general appreciation of the spoken and written word. Courses in speech, phonetics, diction, and delivery helped her to recognize her own talents and led her to deeper appreciation of the nature of words and of how speech enhances them. Above all, she valued Hunter College for increasing her capacity to appreciate the richness of the human experience and for encouraging her to continue to explore herself. While still a student, Ruby married blues singer Frankie Dee Brown in 1941. She adopted his middle name as her stage name. The marriage did not last; the couple was divorced in 1945. She began to appear in radio plays and worked for a short time as a translator for an import business, using her fluency in French and Spanish.

In February 1946 Ruby made her Broadway debut in Robert Ardrey's *Jeb*, a drama about the frustrations of a returning Black war hero. Its star was Ossie Davis. A few months later, she appeared in Philip Yordan's *Anna Lucasta*, with Ossie Davis in an all-Black Broadway production about a streetwalker redeemed by true love. Ruby and Ossie were married in December 1948. Ruby's film debut was in *The Jackie Robinson Story*, directed by Alfred E. Green in 1950. In 1957, she played Sidney Poitier's wife in a waterfront drama, *Edge of the City*, directed by Martin Ritt. Ruby continued to perform on stage throughout the fifties and sixties. She won acclaim for her Broadway performance as Ruth Younger in Lorraine Hansberry's *A Raisin in the Sun* in 1959, and she also won very positive reviews for her role in the 1961 film version of the play. Ruby's acting career included stage, film, and television.

Ruby Dee and Ossie Davis became political activists in the 1950s when their friend Paul Robeson, singer, actor, and civil rights activist, lost his passport for denouncing American involvement in the Korean War. They were also galvanized by the Rosenberg trial, which sentenced Julius and Ethel Rosenberg to death for spying for the Soviet Union. Ruby spoke at a rally against the death penalty in Carnegie Hall. They performed at the 1963 March on Washington along with Pete Seeger, Odetta, Mahalia Jackson, Bob Dylan, Joan Baez, and Peter, Paul, and Mary. They supported the NAACP, the Congress of Racial Equality, the Student Nonviolent Coordinating Committee, and the Southern Christian Leadership Conference, all major civil rights organizations leading the movement in the South.

To help young Black women become established as actors, they founded the Ruby Dee Scholarship in Dramatic Art.

In 1987, Ruby published her memoir, *My One Good Nerve.* The book deals with love, politics, murder, race, spousal abuse, racism, hope, and work. Her readings from the book, including one at Hunter College, won national attention. In 1995, President Bill Clinton awarded Ruby Dee and Ossie Davis the National Medal of Arts. Ruby Dee died in 2014.

During the war years, Hunter students continued to contribute their thoughts and feelings about generational differences within immigrant families, poverty, and racism to the *Echo.* In October 1943, Ethel Frank, a member of the *Echo* staff, who, like Ruby Dee, graduated in 1944, shared her thoughts about the difficulties faced by poor immigrant college students to communicate their struggles to their hardworking parents. In her story, "By Bread Alone," Ethel describes the protagonist thinking about her parents: "She could not tell them that . . . she was lost in a flood of darkness and confusion. And there was no one to whom she could go to for an answer." She knew that her father would have given a part of his being for the opportunity to study that she had now. As she left her crowded home to study at the New York Public Library, she knew that she would never give up seeking to understand the world. She also feared that her desperate loneliness would never leave her.

In the spring 1945 issue of the *Echo*, Antholus Palmos, the coeditor of the magazine, contributed a story, "Guided Tour," that demonstrated the strong desire of a student from a poor family to become culturally literate like her high school friends who were from more affluent backgrounds. Having heard about the Metropolitan Museum of Art from her teacher, but never having been there, Mary decided to go alone in preparation for going with her class. Mary could not explain her desire to go to the museum to her sister, Rose, whose response to Mary's efforts to learn more was an angry rebuke: "I never had to go to museums. . . . That's what you get for being snooty and going to that ritzy school." This lack of family support was experienced by some Hunter students from poor families.

The same issue of the *Echo* carried an essay by Joan Robinson, managing editor, class of 1946, "Don't Take It for Granted." Robinson was an Indianapolis native from a comfortable family for whom racism was a critically important topic. Robinson explained that in her hometown she and her friends met no Blacks, except as servants, as they were not welcome in white theaters, restaurants, swimming pools, and tennis courts. Blacks did not attend white schools or fill jobs above those of porters, cooks, and day laborers. The most disturbing factor in the whole situation: "We did not know that it was discrimination." Robinson's essay pointed to the effect of racism on the victims as well as on those who practiced discrimination.

Echoing the sentiments of President Shuster, Robinson concluded: "In our lives at Hunter we do not continuously suffer from the degradation of discrimination. We are fortunate, but we cannot afford to take our good fortune passively for granted. . . . We are entitled to our equality of opportunity, not through merely accepting it, but through continually implementing its extension to other people. . . . We must start now. Our thinking and our acting will be among the decisive factors in avoiding the disillusionment and despair which followed the first World War."

Robinson contributed two additional essays to the *Echo* that introduced a new topic—the Cold War. Her work demonstrates a keen understanding of politics and her commitment to activism. In December 1945, she wrote an editorial in which she lamented the continuing danger of fascism in the United States, pointing out that those who sympathize with fascist ideologies are still active in spreading their ideas through vehicles of antiminority, anti-Soviet, and anti-trade-union propaganda. Some speak about the inevitability of a third world war. She concluded: "We are citizens as well as students. As citizens, our future is at stake. In our answer to the challenge of American fascism lies the answer to whether or not we shall live out our lives in freedom and security."

In April 1946, Robinson wrote "Your College and You." In this astute piece the young sociologist explained that the *Echo* had planned to devote the editorial columns of the issue entirely to educational questions and the problems of Hunter students. However, as they went to press the issue of world peace had become so acute that the editors decided to add a preface to the discussion with a sharp critique of newspapers that were anti-Soviet. Headlines spelling out Red, Communist, Spy in two-inch high letters strive for an emotional reaction of panic, fear, and hatred. She asked: "Who are these people who would have us go to war again?" She responded: "As college students, we have the obligation to approach this problem sanely and rationally. . . . The Soviet Union is not a mystery. Its citizens are human beings with a determination for peace and security as profound as ours. . . . We must be strong and vocal in expression of our opposition to any and every statement and policy which creates international ill-humor and distrust."

Having set the stage for the need to educate college students, Robinson explained the challenge facing Hunter College. The Board of Higher Education expected fifteen thousand veterans to enroll in the public colleges of New York. She feared that several thousand women would be denied admission unless additional funds and facilities were provided immediately. She called on the state government as well as the city government to meet the challenge. She called for the establishment of a free state university; the State University of New York (SUNY) was founded in 1948. She urged a law to deny tax exemption to all schools that established quotas based on race, color, or creed; informal quotas remained through the coming decades. The editorial ended with a call to students to let their legislators in Albany know their opinions: "There is no dividing line between student problems, national problems and international problems. You and your college can live and develop only within an expanding and healthy world democracy."

In February 1945 Hunter College celebrated its Diamond Jubilee, seventy-five years as a college for women. *The New York Times* announced a two-day program, beginning with a commemorative exhibit at the New York Public Library, where so many Hunter students did research. Speakers included Mayor Fiorello La Guardia; Franklin F. Hopper, director of the New York Public Library; Ordway Tead, chairman of the Board of Higher Education; the president of the Hunter Alumnae Association, Ruth Lewinson; and the president of Hunter, George N. Shuster.

In a brochure created for the event, President Shuster noted that Hunter alumnae numbered close to forty thousand women. Most lived in New York, others contributed around the world. Many were teachers and school administrators, while others held varied positions: accountants, chemists, engineers, doctors, lawyers, librarians, translators, photographers, engravers, dancers, singers, psychologists, traffic managers, social workers, teachers, professors, painters, and designers. Hunter announced an essay contest in honor of the jubilee. Three categories of contestants were invited to participate: college and university students in the United States; teachers in colleges, universities, high schools, and elementary schools in the United States; and high school students in the five boroughs of New York City. Hunter students and faculty were not eligible to compete. Prize money totaling $12,000 in Victory Bonds was contributed by the Lane Bryant Stores. The essay topics reflected the concerns of Hunter administration, faculty, and students: How can American colleges or other social institutions promote appreciation of the cultures of other peoples and cooperation among them? How can the American teacher help to foster intercultural relations? How can national unity be promoted by high schools or other social activity groups?

The judges for the essays were announced in the *Times*: Mrs. Mary McLeod Bethune, president, National Council of Negro Women; Everett R. Clinchy, president, National Conference of Christians and Jews; Alvin Johnson, president emeritus, New School for Social Research; Jerome G. Kerwin, professor of government, University of Chicago; R. A. McGowan, director, Department of Social Action, National Catholic Welfare Conference; Judge Joseph M. Proskauer, president, American Jewish Committee; Miss Rose Schneiderman, president, New York Women's Trade Union League; Honorable G. Howland Shaw, former assistant secretary of state; Mrs. Arthur Hayes Sulzberger, *The New York Times*. Entries were to be submitted by March 1, 1946. Winners would be announced on May 15, 1946. The top prize in each category was $1,000.

Hunter College was in the news for another reason. In 1943 President Shuster and Benno Lee, an Austrian impresario, had established the Hunter College Concert Bureau. A poster was placed above Lee's office declaring: "Music Does More Than Soothe the Savage Beast—It is the medium through which the ordinary human being can communicate with the mind of a genius." In its first year the Saturday Night Celebrity Series presented concerts by Vladimir Horowitz, Yehudi Menuhin, Jan Peerce, and Lotte Lehmann, and a lecture by Thomas Mann. The second year, these performers returned and were joined by Ezio Pinza. In 1945, Jascha Heifetz, Rudolf Firkusny, Erica Morini, and the New York Philharmonic led by Bruno Walter were featured. The list continued to grow in the late forties and throughout the fifties. Zino Francescati, Lauritz Melchior, Nathan Milstein, Arthur Rubenstein, and Isaac Stern made Hunter's Assembly Hall the preferred venue for over eighteen hundred subscribers by 1964.

One of the graduates of the diamond jubilee year was Anita Arrow (Summers). Anita was born in 1925 in Great Neck, Long Island, to immigrant Jewish parents from Romania. She was raised in Manhattan following the stock market crash in 1929 that led to the Depression. Both of her parents valued education very highly. Her older brother, Kenneth J. Arrow, attended City College and won the Nobel Prize in Economics in 1972. Anita attended Hunter College where she was mentored by two women, Professor Dorothy Lampen, the chairman of the Economics Department, and Professor Margaret Spahr, who taught constitutional law in the Political Science Department. Anita was so enthusiastic about the law that she told Professor Spahr she intended to go to law school. Spahr urged her to rethink her plan, telling her that she would get into a good law school, but would be put in a back room of a law firm. Professor Lampen encouraged her to study economics; she chose that field.

Anita remembered the honors course she took that was devoted to John Maynard Keynes. Each student was responsible to report on one chapter of his famous book, *The General Theory of Employment, Interest, and Money*, published in 1936. Anita was to speak about the natural rate of unemployment, a topic of particular interest to all who had lived through the Depression years. She discussed Keynes's view that serious unemployment rates would not quickly end, that equilibrium would not quickly be reached, and that there was a role for government in addressing unemployment. In the honors class, each student was responsible for leading a two-hour session, with frequent requests from the professor for further explanation and for clarity. Focus on presentation skills was an important part of the course. The class had a strong influence on Anita's professional life.

Anita was awarded membership in Phi Beta Kappa and graduated in 1945. She received her MA degree from the University of Chicago in 1947 and was soon hired by Standard Oil as their first female economist. The head of the research department explained that he had hired her because "we decided we could get the same brains for less money." Anita was pleased to be told that she "had the same brains" and was not yet concerned about earning less. While she was at Standard Oil, she began her PhD at Columbia. Anita married Robert Summers who was teaching economics at Yale in 1953. She moved to New Haven and stopped working in 1954 when the first of her three sons was born.

Anita Summers spent a decade raising her children. The family moved to Pennsylvania following her husband's appointment as a faculty member at the University of Pennsylvania. For several years Anita did volunteer work for the League of Women Voters. A call from Swarthmore College asking her to substitute for a professor who died suddenly brought her into the classroom. This was followed by a call from the Federal Reserve Bank of Philadelphia, asking if she would join the urban section of their research department. She worked there for nearly ten years until the University of Pennsylvania asked her to become the founding chairman of Wharton's public policy and management department, the first at a business school.

In her classes at Wharton, Summers applied the personal attention used by Professor Lampen at Hunter. In her public policy class, she gave each of the seventy students twenty minutes to discuss their paper topics.

She helped them focus on a specific question, just as she had been taught in her honors class.

Summers continued to do research through the 1980s and 1990s, writing a series of articles about the postindustrial economy of southeastern Pennsylvania. She didn't lament vanishing industries, but rather encouraged policymakers to explore new economic sectors. She had a strong interest in zoning laws and how they influenced economic growth. In education policy she took a controversial stand advocating merit pay for teachers based on student test scores. Summers died in October 2023.

In October 1945, following the victory celebrations, President Shuster addressed Hunter students with great sympathy and understanding.

> And so when we think of education today I believe we are asking a very grave question indeed. It is not primarily how does one prepare for citizenship? Or, how does one go about training for a job? Or, how can one come most easily by what is in the best books—the hundred more or less—which have sometime been written? It is a far more solemn primitive query than that. It is in Wordsworth's phrase, how can we make the universe habitable?

Shuster ended his talk with his conviction that Hunter students had the power to bring about positive change in the world. He urged them to remember Emerson's line: "The world is built on ideas, not on cotton and iron."

Two years later, sensing continuing malaise among Hunter students, President Shuster addressed them in the 1947 *Wistarion*: "I understand completely how bewildered a young person must be when, standing at the rim of the arena wherein life is acted out, she looks about in vain for something to do which has either intrinsic significance or relationship to the play as a whole. . . . There is then a great work of healing to be done." He called on them to remember great women leaders of the past and to see themselves as worthy successors.

> I hope that each and every one of you will take it as earnestly as Jane Addams or Harriet Martineau or Catherine of Siena took it in her time. It is not exaggerating your importance in the least to say that the decisive query of our time is not what

> happens to the atom bomb, but what happens to the college woman of America. She can't help it. She is the collective queen of the modern age. Upon how she wears her crown and scepter all depends. The women of the rest of the world, sitting with their children in cold and hungry rooms, understood this fully. I hope that you will too, and that nothing will dissuade you from justice, from kindness, and from honesty.

Hunter students did not disappoint. They described themselves in the *Wistarion* as the most heterogeneous group of human beings, as far as race and religion was concerned, as could be found anywhere. They were proud of the spirit of congeniality that was real and spontaneous at Hunter. They wondered if such harmony would be found in the business world. They concluded: "We believe that it is important for us to remember the way things were at college. It is up to us to hold on to the ideals we acquired at college. The contentment and satisfaction of our years after graduation will depend a good deal on how we keep faith with those ideals." One of the students who lived those ideals was Elaine Small (Klein) who was born in 1928. The Small family, Elaine, her parents, and her older brother lived in a three-room apartment in the Bronx. Elaine's father died when she was ten years old. Her mother went to work to support the family. Elaine worked as a child dancer, performing at weddings and parties, contributing her earnings to the family budget. She tap-danced and sang, earning $25 a weekend. During the war, when Elaine was in high school, her mother worked at the Brooklyn Navy Yard and her brother joined the Marine Corps.

Elaine graduated at sixteen and enrolled in Hunter College in 1944. To earn money, she worked on Thursday nights and Saturdays at B. Altman's department store. She majored in speech and theatre, minored in English and physical education. She attended a memorial service in the Assembly Hall for President Roosevelt and remembered listening to Professor Arthur L. Woehl, the chairman of her department, recite "When Lilacs Last in the Dooryard Bloom'd," which was Walt Whitman's tribute to Abraham Lincoln. She participated in many performances, acting or directing. She chaired the lyrics committee for SING during her junior year where she learned about the importance of cooperation, of meeting deadlines, and how to be a stage manager. She also built sets, climbed ladders, and positioned lights.

Some of those skills were useful when she was hired to work backstage in the Playhouse (later the Sylvia and Danny Kaye Playhouse) and in the Assembly Hall, which were rented by professional theatre groups like the Yiddish Theatre, the American Negro Theatre, and Harvard's Hasty Pudding Club, in the late forties and fifties. In addition to professional theatre groups, the Assembly Hall continued to feature Hunter's Concert Series featuring world-class musical talent. The program for 1947–1948 included such luminaries as Serge Koussevitzky, conducting the Boston Symphony Orchestra, and soloists Isaac Stern, Rudolf Serkin, Ezio Pinza, Yehudi Menuhin, Artur Schnabel, Lotte Lehmann, and Arthur Rubinstein.

When Elaine graduated in June 1948, she and two classmates were asked to stay on as teaching fellows in the Department of Speech and Theatre. She began to take MA classes at Hunter. The following summer, she followed the advice of her favorite professor, Charles Elson, who urged his students to travel. She booked passage on a converted troop ship and went to Europe. Later, at the suggestion of one of her classmates, she took courses at Columbia and ultimately completed a PhD. While working on her doctorate, she taught at nearby Marymount Manhattan College, married, and had two children.

After several years of teaching at Marymount, Klein became the chairman of her department. To her surprise, she was later asked to assume the position of academic dean. Klein was the first Jewish dean of a Catholic college, where she taught future Congresswoman Geraldine Ferraro and hosted Coretta Scott King, widow of Martin Luther King Jr. She later found her academic home at Westchester Community College, where she was a professor of English, speech, and communications, as well as president of the Faculty Senate. She was a founding member of the Tri State Consortium for Educational TV. Following in the footsteps of Helen Gray Cone, she focused on the ESL (English as Second Language) challenges of students. Using new technology, she produced pronunciation videos. Klein died in 2016.

During the decade that stretched from 1939 to 1949, all Hunter students experienced the challenges of war and the continuing challenges of peace. They benefited from the leadership of President Shuster, from professional and caring faculty, and from the guidance of Hunter alumnae. Graduates of this decade turned their attention to a wide variety of professional pursuits. In the arts, Hunter educated a future opera diva, a Broadway star, a world-renowned dancer, and an architectural journalist/

historian; in the social sciences, Hunter educated a future congresswoman and an economist; in the sciences, Hunter educated a Nobel prize-winning physicist, a renowned ichthyologist, and an eminent physician. Hunter continued to educate teachers at all levels from elementary school to university.

Chapter Five

"A Natural Training Ground for Feminism" (1950–1964)

After the end of World War II, women who had worked in a wide variety of war industries were encouraged to go home, to leave their jobs so that returning veterans could find employment. However, as the aspirations and careers of Hunter College students and graduates of this period demonstrate, Hunter women continued to be motivated by the well-established culture of their school; they strove to achieve academic excellence and to participate in civic action. Pauli Murray, who had graduated in 1933, reflected in her memoirs that Hunter College was "a natural training ground for feminism." She explained, "Having a faculty and student body in which women assumed leadership reinforced our egalitarian values, inspired our confidence in the competence of women generally, and encouraged our resistance to subordinate roles." Many graduates of the fifties followed in the footsteps of Julia Richman by becoming "the first" to achieve a leadership role; some, like Rosalyn Yalow, opened new fields of study that hadn't yet erected barriers to women; others, like Marion Wilson Starling, challenged academic dogma to create new ways to understand the world. Hunter women of the 1950s stood firmly and consciously on the shoulders of the graduates of the preceding decades and built on their achievements.

Some of the early graduates continued to hold important positions in the college: Professor Edna Wells Luetz, class of 1915, chaired the Art Department from 1948 until 1963; Professor E. Adelaide Hahn, also class of 1915, chaired the Classics Department for thirty-seven years, until 1963; Professor Augusta Neidhardt, class of 1912, founded and chaired the Physical Education Department until 1958. These women had helped to build the culture of the college for decades from their positions on the faculty and as leaders in the Associate Alumnae. Mina Rees, class of 1923, returned to Hunter College in 1953 as a professor and dean of the faculty after working to support the war effort, followed by years of distributing government funding to build scientific research programs at major American universities. She joined another Hunter alumna and longtime member of the faculty, Ruth Goldstein Weintraub, class of 1925, in applying social science methodology to improve the services provided to Hunter students.

There were twenty-three departments in the college in 1950; twelve were chaired by women and eleven by men. The women included some who had been educated in different institutions, bringing new ideas to the college. Professor Mary Latimer Gambrell, chairman of the History Department, would later serve briefly as president of Hunter. Gambrell, from South Carolina, attained her BA at Greenville Woman's College and her MA and PhD at Columbia. In 1950 she introduced a new course on world events, 1750–1950, in fifty-year sequences over four semesters. Professor Jewell Bushey, chairman of the Mathematics Department, received her BA at the University of Arkansas, her MA at the University of Missouri, and her PhD at the University of Chicago. She continued the tradition of leadership pioneered by Emma Requa. Professor Marjorie Anderson, a graduate of Smith College, also received her PhD at the University of Chicago. Building on the tradition established by Helen Gray Cone, she chaired the English Department, the largest at Hunter College. Professor Anna Jacobson received her PhD in German literature from the University of Bonn. She became chairman of the German Department, the smallest in the college, and organized Hunter's Goethe bicentennial convocation in 1950, the only observance in New York City of the two hundredth anniversary of the poet's birth. Thomas Mann attended and spoke on Goethe and democracy. Professor Madge McKinney, born in Rome, Ohio, completed her BA and MA at Western Reserve University and her PhD at Columbia. She chaired the Political Science Department and ran the Model Congress program for sixteen New York City high schools. Honors students in her department worked with city agencies. The chairman of the Sociology and Anthropology Department, Professor Agnes Byrnes, received her BA from Northwestern, her MA from Columbia, and her PhD from Bryn Mawr. She continued the tradition of maintaining a strong relationship with the American Museum of Natural History. She added internships with public welfare agencies in New York City to prepare students for jobs after graduation. Professor Marguerite E. Jones, class of 1911 at Hunter, did graduate work at the University of Vermont and Columbia. She chaired the Department of Speech and Dramatics, introducing a radio workshop where students could air and record programs. She also created an opportunity for students to gain experience in the Long Island Medical Hospital speech clinic. Hunter College offered employment to women faculty who were educated all over the United States.

Hunter students had multiple opportunities to witness women leaders at work as deans, as department chairs, and as faculty. Florence Rosenfeld (Howe), who graduated in 1950, was one of the many students whose life was changed by her Hunter experience. Florence was born in 1929 in Brooklyn. Her parents, Samuel, a taxi driver, and Frances, a bookkeeper, and her brother, Jack, lived in a very small apartment. Florence slept on a cot in the hallway and shared a dresser in her brother's tiny bedroom. She did her homework on a used typewriter at the kitchen table. Her hardworking mother warned her to expect a life of poverty. Nevertheless, she encouraged Florence to be studious. Her mother hoped she would become a teacher and would thus have a steady source of income.

Florence enrolled at Hunter College High School in January 1943. She was immediately told to report to the speech therapist who arranged for her to have lessons three days a week after school. She began to hear the difference between her voice and diction and that of her classmates. She knew that if she began to sound like them her family would make fun of her "hoity-toity" accent. She practiced every day, but it took more than a year to erase the Brooklyn working-class accent.

Florence had wanted to attend Ohio State and was prepared to earn enough money to support most of her needs. She asked her mother to contribute $300 for her first year. Her mother denied the request, reminding Florence that Hunter College offered free tuition; the registration fee in 1946 was eight dollars per term, and books were included in the fee. Despite her disappointment in not going away to college, Florence recorded in her memoir being awed by the Park Avenue building that became her academic home for four years. She described the colossus of beautiful white stone with new marble floors, a grand auditorium, spacious elevators, and sunlit classrooms to her quiet father. She spoke about Roosevelt House, the former residence of Eleanor and Franklin Roosevelt, which housed religious clubs and social organizations. Florence also tried to explain the inspirational college motto, *Mihi cura futuri*, to her father.

Florence was the first member of her family to attend college. She planned to become a high school biology teacher. As a freshman, she registered for the required English class as well as for German, physiology, and American history. She planned to take math and chemistry the following year. She recalled her feelings that first year: "Almost at once, I knew I was in a place that felt welcoming, even comfortable, that I was with people who shared my story, or if they did not, could accept my differences. I looked forward to my classes and to being in the new building. I didn't want to leave at the end of the day, though I knew I had to go to my part-time job, since I was determined to buy my own clothes."

The first semester of American history, however, proved deeply disappointing. The professor lectured interminably about the four gospels. Florence took notes diligently but wondered what the gospels had to do with American history. She never asked a question; the rest of the class was silent too. Finally, after weeks of building frustration, Florence and four other students headed to the cafeteria to talk about the class. The group was concerned that they were not learning the appropriate subject matter and would therefore not be prepared for the following semester's work. They nominated Florence and another student to speak to Dean Ann Anthony. Florence described Anthony, who had graduated from Hunter when it was still the Normal College in 1904, and had taught pedagogy at Hunter from 1911, getting her MA and PhD from NYU, as "a motherly looking woman in an elegant dark suit and white blouse." She had gray hair softly styled around her smiling face. She was quite beautiful, calm, and gracious. Florence explained the concerns of the group of students she represented who worried that the term was half over, and they were still reading Matthew, Mark, Luke, and John. Dean Anthony said she was glad that they had come to see her and assured them that following midterm, the class would get to American history. Years later, Florence understood that her professor was offering the class, which had many Jewish students, what she thought they would need to understand the Puritans. Florence got her only C in that class. A's in English, German, and physiology put her on the dean's list.

Florence began to go to lunch in the cafeteria with students she met in her classes. By the end of the semester a small diverse group—Harriet Kilpatrick (Black), Mickie DeSantis (Catholic), Lois Trencher, Millie Trachtenberg, Joyce Cohen, and Florence (all four Jewish), decided to form the first interracial and interreligious House Plan. A year later the group reestablished themselves as Alpha Omega Pi, a diverse sorority. Their statement of purpose was included in their constitution: "To provide an opportunity for girls of all races, religions, and cultural backgrounds to live, work, and maintain social relations on an equal level." Dean Anthony supported their efforts.

In her sophomore year, Florence took Introduction to Sociology taught by Professor Mary H. Diggs, one of very few Black faculty at Hunter. Diggs read aloud from the works of Columbia University social psychologist Otto Klineberg, including his book, *Negro Intelligence and Selective Migration*. This class motivated Florence to try to change her parents' views of racial difference. Florence brought her Black sorority sister, Harriet Kilpatrick, home for dinner. She was invited to Harriet's home for a similar reason. Florence was not successful in changing her parents' views. More and more, she distanced herself from her family. The college

Figure 5.1. Florence Rosenfeld (Howe), at right, Student Council president, 1949. *Source*: Archives and Special Collections, Hunter College Libraries, Hunter College of the City University of New York, New York City.

became her home. She explained: "It is difficult to capture the feelings of joy I experienced entering the building each day or walking over to Roosevelt House for a meeting. . . . In Hunter's halls and classrooms I felt competent as well as accomplished." Though her science teachers felt she was not skilled in science and math they encouraged her to follow her excellent grades to a career in the humanities.

Florence became the chair of the Elections Committee as a sophomore and as a junior she was elected president of the Student Council. In that role she had public responsibilities, including speaking to large audiences. She was insecure about speaking on the stage of the Assembly Hall, but she loved being assigned a desk, a closet, and a bulletin board in one of the rooms allocated to student officers and editors. This room was her first private space. Florence went to classes in the mornings, to her part-time job in the afternoon, to the cafeteria for dinner, and then she worked on her papers and on college business in her office, returning to Brooklyn when her father was out driving his taxi, and her mother and brother were asleep.

Florence continued to excel in her classes and was elected to Phi Beta Kappa at the end of her junior year. Her mother was not impressed by her accomplishment. In her senior year, she took a class with Professor Hoxie Neale Fairchild who urged her to go to graduate school. Anticipating her interests, Fairchild warned her that women writers were not important enough to study. She took President Shuster's seventeenth-century poetry seminar. He also counseled her to go to graduate school. Florence reported their advice to her mother who replied: "Those people, why don't they mind their own business?" Ultimately, her mother agreed to allow her to go to graduate school if she first took summer classes in stenography, in case the graduate program did not work out.

In her last semester, Florence had personal troubles and went to see Dean Anthony again. Florence had wed the soldier she had corresponded with throughout her college years. Three months after the wedding she was certain that she had made a terrible mistake. She left home in the middle of the night and went back to her parents' apartment, but they insisted she return to her husband. Dean Anthony agreed to help. She telephoned the "Y" and arranged for a room for a week, until she could find Florence a job with housing. She loaned her some money. Eventually Florence's mother and her estranged husband met with Dean Anthony and were persuaded to annul the marriage.

Figure 5.2. Dean Ann Anthony, 1953. *Source*: Archives and Special Collections, Hunter College Libraries, Hunter College of the City University of New York, New York City.

At graduation, Florence received the Roosevelt Memorial Award for service to Hunter College, a cash prize of $250, enough to pay for books and expenses for a year of graduate studies at Smith College, which had awarded her $1,250 to cover tuition, room, and board. Florence credited Hunter as the place where she learned to think. She also understood that one could make mistakes and recover from them. In 1951 she received her MA in English from Smith College. In 1954 she began doctoral studies at the University of Wisconsin in art history and literature. In 1960 she was hired as a faculty member at Goucher College, a private women's college in Maryland.

In the summer of 1964, Florence joined hundreds of students and faculty who went to Mississippi to teach in Freedom Schools. Florence went to Jackson, Mississippi, and wrote an essay about her experience that was included in a book published that year, *Myths of Coeducation*. The essay, "Mississippi Freedom Schools: The Politics of Education," was reprinted the following year in the *Harvard Education Review*. It explained her ideas about education, race, politics, and feminism. Three years later, she declared her intent not to pay income taxes to protest US involvement in Vietnam.

During the 1950s and 1960s Florence married three times, permanently taking the last name Howe, the name of one of her husbands. In 1970, Florence Howe founded the Feminist Press, a nonprofit organization established to advance women's rights and to amplify feminist perspectives. From 1972 to 1982, Howe assisted in editing the *Women's Studies Quarterly*. As an author, editor, publisher, and literary scholar, Howe continued to nurture the new field of women's studies. She taught classes in the field at Hofstra College (now University), at Queens College, at Goucher College, and at SUNY Old Westbury. She lectured widely about women's studies, especially during her term as president of the Modern Language Association. She created opportunities for hundreds of women writers to publish their works and for thousands of readers to read them. She also reprinted important works by women authors that were long out of print, refuting Professor Fairchild's warning to eschew topics about women writers. Florence Howe died in 2020 having reissued the works of many forgotten women authors and published the works of new women writers.

In 1951, one year after Florence graduated as an English major, Mildred Spiewak (Dresselhaus) graduated as a physics major. Mildred was born in 1930, the younger of two children, the daughter of Polish Jewish immigrants in Brooklyn. Her father worked as a laborer when he was physically able. As he was chronically ill, the family relied on relief payments to make ends meet. Her mother worked at menial jobs while Mildred was in school. Though her parents had little formal education and struggled to make ends meet, they placed a high value on education. When Mildred was three, they moved to the Bronx to live near a violin teacher who offered free lessons to her brother, Irving, a musical prodigy. Within a few months of their move, the teacher died. In recognition of Irving's talent, a music school in Manhattan agreed to provide scholarships for both children. Thus, Mildred spent every Saturday studying violin from the age of five. She learned to read music before she could read words. She continued to study music for eight years.

For Mildred, the weekly musical interlude provided a refuge from her uninspiring elementary school where classes were large and unruly, and teachers were focused on maintaining order. Her neighborhood was run by gangs; Mildred was not permitted to play outdoors unless one of her parents was present to ensure her safety. Irving was promoted four grades above his age group as he was a prodigy in many subjects. Soon, he was accepted at the Bronx High School of Science and became part of a new world. It was through Irving that Mildred learned of competitive entrance exams to selective high schools in New York City. Only one of those schools, HCHS, was open to girls. No one from her school had ever taken the test. Mildred's teachers counseled her not to waste time on the possibility of winning acceptance. Despite the lack of support, she wrote to HCHS to ask for copies of previous exams, studied books borrowed from her local library, and passed. She was the first from her school to attend HCHS.

At HCHS Mildred's classmates were from middle-income families whose parents had goals beyond mere survival for their children. Mildred acculturated to her new environment. She had no trouble in science and math classes, but she struggled for two years to meet the high standards in English and history. Mildred also became active in a variety of school clubs and played in the school orchestra. Her abilities were appreciated by her teachers. Recognizing that Mildred needed to earn money, they advised her of opportunities to tutor. Mildred had tutored neighborhood children for fifty cents an hour since she was in the sixth grade. Her HCHS teachers told her to charge $5 an hour to her new pupils. Her reputation as a tutor soared. Mildred's earnings from tutoring helped her family to survive.

The teachers at HCHS expected all their students to be successful academically and to go on to productive careers. Though her brother had continued his education after high school, going to Cooper Union and later to pursue a doctorate at the Massachusetts Institute of Technology (MIT), Mildred's parents had no plan for her to go to college. Fortunately, there was no need for her to apply to college as she was automatically admitted to Hunter College following her graduation from HCHS in 1947. Having been a successful tutor for many years, Mildred assumed she would become a teacher and planned to take some pedagogy classes.

During her sophomore year, she took an advanced physics class taught by Rosalyn Yalow. The class was very small, about six students.

Mildred excelled in the class. Professor Yalow noticed her ability and suggested that she become a professional physicist. Mildred remembered her saying, "Why don't you do the same as I'm doing? You can do it too." As a result, Mildred decided to go to graduate school to become a physicist. She didn't have a clear idea of what it meant to pursue a career in physics. She explained that her objective in going to college was to get some training so that she could do something better than work in a zipper factory, which was a job she had one summer.

By the time she decided to become a physicist, Mildred was no longer worried about earning a living; she had continued to tutor throughout college and was able to save some of the money she had earned. Her professors urged her to apply to graduate school, but her parents were worried about a commitment to additional schooling. As was typical for parents in the postwar years, they wanted their daughter to marry and to have children. Mildred took the advice of her professors and applied to graduate schools as well as to the Fulbright Foundation. Mildred graduated from Hunter *summa cum laude* in 1951 and was elected to Phi Beta Kappa. Her graduation speaker was Mina Rees. After the ceremony, the Hunter alumna of 1923 spoke to Mildred and encouraged her to attend Cambridge University. Mildred was touched by her interest. Years later, her assessment of her Hunter experience was insightful. She praised the college for teaching her about the responsibility of individuals to society. She described the Hunter ethic as one of a lot of personal attention to individual students, which celebrated self-starting, initiative, and the idea of serving society.

Rosalyn Yalow, Hunter's first physics graduate, advised Mildred to study physics at a top graduate school, and she wrote letters of recommendation for admission to such schools. Mildred spent a year at Cambridge University on a Fulbright fellowship and then a year at Harvard. When she began her doctoral studies at the University of Chicago, she was twenty-two years old. Though her advisor believed that educating women was a waste of time and money, Mildred was fortunate to study with Enrico Fermi. She judged him a fantastic teacher and copied one of his techniques when she began to teach. Fermi always distributed lecture notes to his students so that they didn't have to copy down equations from the board, risking error. Mildred did the same. He also made a point of getting to know each of his students, inviting them to his home for social evenings. Mildred followed his example. In 1958 she defended her thesis and married Eugene Dresselhaus. She followed him to Cornell where he was an assistant professor, and she had a postdoc. In 1960 both Gene and Mildred accepted positions at the Lincoln Laboratory operated by MIT. While at Lincoln, she gave birth to her four children.

Mildred was asked to work in the newly emerging field of magneto-optics and decided to use semimetals, chemical elements that exhibit the properties of both metals and nonmetals, as her materials system. She also studied the electronic structure of graphite and the other semimetals. Her work contributed significantly to the fundamental foundations of condensed matter physics studies on these semimetals. In 1967, Mildred was invited to hold the Abby Rockefeller Mauzé visiting professorship at MIT. After a few months she was invited to be a full professor of electrical engineering, to teach classes, and to train graduate students for research careers in industry and academia.

Mildred became a leader in the study of the electrical and electronic properties of solids, specializing in nanoscience, the physics of materials at scales of one-billionth of a meter. Like many Hunter graduates, she achieved several firsts. She was the first woman to serve as a tenured full professor at MIT and the first woman to win the National Medal of Science for engineering. She was known as the "queen of carbon" in recognition of her efforts to understand and develop newer, stronger, more technologically useful carbon molecules. In addition to her scientific research, Mildred was active in encouraging the development of women as scientists. She and a colleague organized the first Women's Forum at MIT to explore the role of women in science. Two years later she won a Carnegie Foundation grant to further that cause.

In 2014, President Barack Obama awarded Mildred Dresselhaus the Presidential Medal of Freedom, the country's highest civilian honor. She was the second Hunter alumna to receive the award first won by Antonia Pantoja (see below). Three years later, General Electric broadcast a TV commercial that boasted of their commitment to hire more women. In the commercial little girls play with Millie Dresselhaus dolls and dress up in Millie Dresselhaus wigs and sweaters. The narrator asks: "What if we treated great female scientists like they were stars? What if we treated Millie Dresselhaus the same as any celebrity?" In addition to the honors cited above, Millie Dresselhaus won the Kavli Prize in Nanoscience, the Enrico Fermi Award, and dozens of honorary doctorates. She served as president of the American Physical Society. Following in the footsteps of Mina Rees, Mildred Dresselhaus served as president of the American Association for the Advancement of Science. She died in 2017.

In 1952, one year after Dresselhaus graduated from Hunter, Antonia Pantoja received her Hunter degree. Born in San Juan, Puerto Rico, in June 1922 to an unwed mother, raised by grandparents in the Barrio Obrero, a housing project built for workers, Antonia Pantoja was determined to improve her living conditions. There was no electricity or indoor plumbing in her childhood home. Her grandfather was a skilled laborer working for the American Tobacco Company. Groups of workers discussing plans to form a union often met in their home. He was a leader who was blacklisted for his role in attempting to unionize the company. Following a long strike, the company left Puerto Rico. Pantoja's grandfather died a few years later when she was seven. The family became dependent on the income of her grandmother and aunts who took in laundry to earn money for food.

When Pantoja graduated from the eighth grade she campaigned to attend Central High School. Her grandmother argued that going to high school was a luxury the family could not afford. She was finally persuaded to permit her granddaughter to enroll when she was convinced that Pantoja's slight build would make her unemployable for several years. Most of the children who attended Central High School came from families who could afford to buy them proper clothing and shoes. Pantoja spent hours searching for hard cardboard to cover the holes in her shoes. She got a job in the school cafeteria and covertly brought food home to her hungry family. A few months after she started her studies, she was diagnosed with tuberculosis and sent to a sanitorium for three months. For the first time in her life, she had adequate nutrition and rest.

A few years later, with similar determination, Pantoja raised the funds necessary to attend the University of Puerto Rico. She planned to complete a two-year degree in elementary education. She left the program before completing her studies, as she was offered a teaching job in a one-room rural school. Two years later, in 1944, she sailed with a friend to the United States in search of more education and opportunities. In New York, she became a designer in a lampshade factory and began to observe the living conditions of fellow immigrants from Puerto Rico.

Pantoja entered Hunter College in 1950, majoring in sociology. There she met Maggie Miranda, a Puerto Rican in one of her classes. Through Maggie she soon met several other Puerto Rican students at Hunter. These young women were born in New York and were several years younger than Pantoja; they started meeting in Pantoja's apartment. When the group expanded to include others, it moved to the Good Neighbor Community Center in East Harlem. The meetings began as social and learning sessions. Later, they decided to form a committee to propose a plan of action. Pantoja was chosen president of the Hispanic Young Adult Association, a group that changed its name to the Puerto Rican Association for Community Affairs.

Pantoja graduated from Hunter College in June 1952 having received credit for the classes she took at the University of Puerto Rico. She continued her education at the School of Social Work at Columbia where she was funded by an Antoinette Cannon Foundation Scholarship and a John Jay Whitney Foundation Opportunity Fellowship. Pantoja was critical of social work education at Columbia, which prepared her for an administrative career supervising social workers rather than preparing her to confront the deep poverty and social inequality she found among Puerto Ricans in New York.

In 1961, Pantoja founded the ASPIRA Association, a nonprofit organization that worked with New York City schools to encourage high school Latinos to pursue higher education while simultaneously improving their leadership and organizational skills. ASPIRA was a success in New York City and developed into a national program. In 1972, ASPIRA of New York filed a federal civil rights lawsuit against the New York City Board of Education demanding that the city's schools provide classroom instruction in Spanish as well as in English as a Second Language (ESL). This case helped to establish bilingual education as a norm for non-English-speaking students across the country.

Pantoja played a central role in establishing Boricua College, an academic institution that offered liberal arts programs to Puerto Rican students and to others whose communities were underrepresented in higher education. She was also instrumental in founding the Puerto Rican Research and Resources Center in Washington, DC. Pantoja received her doctorate from Union College in 1973 and joined the faculty at San Diego State University's School of Social Work in 1978. She later founded the Graduate School for Community Development, a private school, teaching skills in community development, economic development, and leadership skills.

In 1996, President Clinton awarded Antonia Pantoja the Presidential Medal of Freedom, the first Hunter graduate (Mildred Dresselhaus was the second) and the first Puerto Rican woman to receive this award. In 2002, Pantoja published a memoir in which she alluded to being a lesbian, having been wary about making that information public for decades. She died several months later and was survived by her partner of many decades, social worker and activist Wilhelmina Perry. Schools in many cities across the country are named for Antonia Pantoja.

In the late 1940s, the *Arrow* replaced the *Bulletin* as the weekly student newspaper. On November 27, 1950, it reported on a lecture given by Howard Fast, a popular writer who was considered a communist by some. Fast warned students about American imperialism in Korea, the Philippines, Java, and six Latin American countries. He explained that the culture of Ralph Waldo Emerson, Henry David Thoreau, Nathaniel Hawthorne, Herman Melville, and Theodore Dreiser was dying and warned that America was viewed as a huge and monstrous murder machine. Invitations to Fast to speak at Columbia and NYU were withdrawn. His invitation to speak again at Hunter on May 16 to a student group, the Young Progressives of America, was honored. *The New York Times* ran an article with the title "Hunter College Head Will Not Ban Author's Appearance," referring to the controversy that had erupted over the invitation.

President Shuster received a telegram from the Joint Committee against Communism, a coalition of New York State groups including the American Legion and the Veterans of Foreign Wars, asking him to prevent the speaker from appearing. The committee protested the use of the tax-supported facility for a speech by Howard Fast. Shuster, who thought Fast was a mediocre writer who employed fuzzy thinking, expressed his belief that students could discover that fact by having an opportunity to hear him speak. President Shuster received a letter of support from Hunter faculty, from the ACLU, and from Harold Taylor, president of Sarah Lawrence College, who explained: "If we begin excluding communists, we will end by excluding anyone who says anything provocative, unorthodox, or interesting."

Several months later, in October, with the controversy still bubbling, President Shuster gave an address about academic freedom to the National Council of Jewish Women. He explained his views on the controversy at Hunter. He thought that there were some older faculty who continued to believe in communism despite the Hitler-Stalin pact and the abolition of civil liberties and religious freedom in the Soviet Union. Shuster saw these faculty as tragic figures who clung to their youthful idealism in the face of the new reality. He didn't perceive their ideas, or those of Howard Fast, as a danger to young students.

President Shuster continued to speak out for civil liberties and against government interference with academic freedom. At a speech to the National Civil Liberties Clearing House in Washington, DC, he called for an investigation of Senator Joseph McCarthy: "I would remind you that the university has always been a forum in the presence of which the lords of the passing hour are subjected to scrutiny. . . . I fancy that the day on which the Senator is summoned before the bar of American history and social science will not be the least revealing of his career." The *Arrow* reported this story in March 1953.

The Board of Higher Education did not share President Shuster's views. In accord with New York State's Feinberg Law, originally passed in 1949, the board created a committee to investigate faculty suspected of membership in the Communist Party. On April 15, 1954, the *Arrow* published a special edition with the banner headline, "THREE HUNTER PROFS SUSPENDED BY BHE [Board of Higher Education]." Permanently suspended following an investigation were Louis Weisner, professor of mathematics for twenty-seven years; Charles W. Hughes, professor of music for twenty-seven years; and Jerauld McGill, professor of psychology and philosophy for twenty-five years. These men were believed to have continued their membership in the Communist Party and were found to have hindered the board's efforts to investigate Communist Party activity at Hunter College. Two other faculty had been suspended previously, in 1952, for refusal to testify before the Senate Internal Security Committee: Bernard Reiss, professor of psychology for twenty-five years, and Henrietta Friedman, professor of Latin for twenty-five years.

The *Arrow* carried a statement by Friedman responding to the question asking whether she was a member of the Communist Party:

> I must refuse to answer that question. . . . I have been teaching for 27 years. . . . I have been a very proud teacher and I have been proud because of the traditions and standards of my profession. One of those traditions is that as long as a teacher does his job in the classroom, as long as he doesn't try to indoctrinate his students, his private opinions are his private opinions, and no one has the right to ask about those opinions. It would be my feeling that if I answered these questions, I would betray the entire teaching profession.

Jay Gorney, a part-time faculty member in the Music Department and composer of the music for the popular Depression-era song "Brother, Can You Spare a Dime?," was also suspended. He testified to the House Un-American Activities Committee. A section of the testimony was printed in the student newspaper: "I got my first education in Poland, in a pogrom, when my father decided to find a land where we could be free—we could have freedom from fear and live a life as a father wants to bring up his children. . . . The Constitution of the United States is a very beautiful thing. . . . The First Amendment came first. Apparently, our Founding Fathers intended that to be the most important thing."

Meryl Fialka, who graduated in January 1954, wrote an opinion piece in the *Arrow* questioning the right of the Board of Higher Education to fire professors based on their membership in the Communist Party. She pointed out that the Communist Party was a legal political party. One could belong to the party without committing a crime. She responded to the growing influence of McCarthyism in America by adding, "Utilization of the tactics which we condemn in other societies cannot possibly strengthen any democratic institutions. . . . We are a constitutional democracy. Let us not deviate from the constitutional democratic methods which set the United States apart from so many countries in the world."

President Shuster continued to struggle with the Board of Higher Education through the fifties. Two editors of the *Arrow*, Ursula Mahoney and Marie Pantuosco, both English majors, class of 1954, reminisced in 1970 about their time at Hunter College: "Witch hunts, Joe McCarthy, the Communist threat—all these were real concerns of the fifties." They felt flanked by McCarthy on the one hand and the Cold War in Europe on the other, while a real war in Korea was beginning to send young men to fight. They knew that they were often called "The Quiet Generation." Nevertheless, they reported that the candidacy of Adlai Stevenson in 1952 created substantial student interest, more than any other candidate they could remember.

The editors of the 1954 *Wistarion* invited Ralph J. Bunche, winner of the Nobel Peace Prize in 1950 and an African American active at a high level in the United Nations, to submit a dedication. His words captured the sentiment of many in the Hunter community and encouraged the graduates to remain hopeful.

> These are difficult and dangerous times, both abroad and at home. . . . I would certainly not wish to minimize in any way the threats to peace, to our freedom and to our way of life. These threats are real. . . . But they should not be exaggerated or exploited in such a way as to stimulate corroding fear amongst us, a people who have always been confident in ourselves and

> in our material and spiritual strength. . . . I am convinced that there is good and sound basis for hope . . . because I know that peoples everywhere wish for peace, and because there is an increasing realization throughout the world that atomic warfare can achieve no results other than the madness of destruction and the black-out of civilization.
>
> I am hopeful about the preservation of freedom in the world because I believe that the people who now enjoy freedom and those very many millions who aspire to it are resolute and determined to preserve and achieve it. . . .
>
> My main concern stems from what appears to be a disturbing trend toward cynicism and despair. . . . There are too many who permit fear to replace confidence, reason to succumb to emotion. I venture to hope that Hunter College will provide few recruits for these ranks.

One of the graduates that year who shared Bunche's optimism was Evelyn Erika Sass (Handler), born in May 1933 in Budapest, Hungary. She was one of four sisters raised by Donald and Ilona Sass, Orthodox Jews. Her parents had two children and adopted two others to ensure their escape from the Nazis. Evelyn was seven years old when her family left Hungary and settled in New York City in 1940, where her parents both found employment as laborers in the garment industry. Finances became tighter after her father's death when Evelyn was a teenager. At HCHS, Evelyn was an academic star. She graduated in 1950 and continued her studies at Hunter College, graduating, *summa cum laude*, in 1954, as a physiology and chemistry major. She earned her MA and PhD in cellular biology at NYU in 1963. She was appointed instructor and lecturer in the Department of Biological Sciences at Hunter while completing her dissertation. In 1965, she was promoted to assistant professor, and she advanced through the ranks to full professor in 1975. Two years later, she was named dean of the Division of Sciences and Mathematics at Hunter.

One of her significant achievements while at Hunter was winning a grant from the National Institutes of Health for a Minority Biomedical Research Support Program. The $1 million grant was designed to increase research participation by minority students in Hunter's science departments and to encourage minority students to pursue biomedical careers. Evelyn continued her own research at the Karolinska Institute in Sweden and at the Sloan Kettering Institute. She and her husband, Eugene Handler, also a biologist, collaborated on leukemia research. Her leukemia research received five major grants from the National Science Foundation and the National Institutes of Health.

In 1980, the Handlers and their two children moved to the University of New Hampshire where Evelyn was inaugurated president. She was the first woman to hold that position, and the first woman named president of a land-grant university in the United States. By the time she left in 1983, she had won $15 million in federal funds for the construction of Morse Hall, the home of the Institute for the Study of Earth, Oceans, and Space at the University of New Hampshire. She had also instituted an honors program and generally raised the national and international reputation of the university.

Her appointment as president of Brandeis University made her one of the first women in the country to preside over a top-tier coeducational university. Brandeis, established in 1948 as a nonsectarian alternative for Jews excluded by quotas from many private American universities, was a highly ranked university when she arrived, but it was struggling with budget deficits and declining applications. Handler was determined to raise money, to renovate dormitories, to improve the sports program, and to diversify the student body, which was about 70 percent Jewish. She ran into a political storm when she instructed the university food service in 1987 to "internationalize" the student cafeteria by adding pork and shellfish to the menu, foods that were staples in the diet of Asian Americans, a demographic she sought to attract. Some trustees protested this move away from traditional Jewish dietary rules.

Handler continued to press for increasing the presence of diverse students; she was met with strong objections from those who wished to keep things the way they were. Despite the controversy, Handler raised $200 million, was successful in laying the groundwork for a business school, a center for human and artificial intelligence research, and the first sports and recreation center on campus. By the time she left, in 1991, students and donors were more diverse. Handler was appointed head of the California Academy of Sciences for several years. In retirement, she returned to New Hampshire where she enrolled in law school at the age of seventy. She graduated in 2006. Five years later she was killed after being hit by a car in a pedestrian crosswalk.

Rita Abrams (Hauser), another stellar Hunter student of the early 1950s, graduated *magna cum laude* in 1954. Rita was born in Brooklyn in 1934 to Nathan and Frieda Abrams; she was the older of two daughters.

Her father was a businessman who was active in Republican politics, supporting Governors Thomas Dewey and Nelson Rockefeller. Rita grew up with an interest in politics. She excelled at Samuel J. Tilden High School and hoped to attend college. Her father, however, was skeptical about higher education for women. He did not agree to Rita's plan to attend Mount Holyoke, so she applied to tuition-free Hunter College. Thinking she might become a teacher he agreed to her enrollment at Hunter. Rita began her studies at Hunter College in 1950. Influenced by the Cold War climate of the times, she decided to major in history and minor in political science. Rita joined the History Club and was elected president. She was also elected vice president of the International Relations Club.

She remembered two history professors, Dorothy Fowler, who taught American history, and Beatrice Hyslop, who taught French history. Both women were serious scholars who had an important influence on Rita. Fowler grew up in Waukesha, Wisconsin; she completed her undergraduate studies at Carroll College and her PhD at the University of Wisconsin. Hyslop received her BA from Mount Holyoke and her PhD from Columbia. Rita was especially interested in Hyslop's lectures on the central issues of the French Revolution. She wondered: Why did people band together and overthrow the regime that they knew? What kind of governance did they form afterward? Did it work? Rita felt that these issues were applicable to all times. Hyslop recommended that Rita plan a career as a historian. But Rita wanted to attend law school and to enter political life. Hyslop entreated her to apply for a Fulbright to spend a year in France. Rita applied, won the fellowship, and spent a year perfecting her French and learning about the plans for a European Common Market. This experience deepened her interest in international affairs and shaped her career choice.

While still an undergraduate, Rita met Eleanor Roosevelt, who was a member of the US delegation to the United Nations until January 1953. Roosevelt needed assistance organizing her papers, some of which were in French. Rita had the necessary skills and began to file the papers. She also spoke to Mrs. Roosevelt about her desire to go to law school and her father's opposition to her plan as he was convinced that there were no women lawyers. Mrs. Roosevelt wrote a letter to Rita's father explaining that Rita was brilliant and would have a fine future as a lawyer. He agreed to let her apply. President Shuster wrote a strong letter of support for her applications to both Harvard and Chicago. Chicago offered her a full scholarship; Harvard offered to pay only for her tuition. She was prepared to attend Chicago, but the dean of the University of Chicago Law School,

Edward Levi, encouraged her to go to Harvard, which had accepted its first woman in 1953. Reasoning that Harvard Law had accepted very few women, while Chicago had many, he told her she would stand out at Harvard. She followed his advice and enrolled at Harvard.

In an oral interview Rita credited Hunter for preparing her well for the challenges of Harvard. She remembered that Hunter faculty noticed her intelligence and encouraged her to succeed. It is unlikely that she knew of Harvard Law's rejection of Pauli Murray and Bella Savitsky (Abzug), who had applied before the law school accepted women. When Rita met the dean of Harvard Law, Erwin Griswold, she faced lingering resentment toward the new policy. Griswald asked her, "What are you doing here?" It took her a few minutes to realize that he was questioning her presence in the law school. She told him that she wanted to be a lawyer, to practice law, and to go into politics. The dean countered: "You women, you won't go through with it, many of you quit. You won't have much of a career." She disagreed, telling him, "I am going to have a real career. It's going to be whatever I want to make of it."

Rita met her husband, Gustave Hauser, at Harvard. He was a law school graduate and Army veteran teaching a class in the law school. They met at a party and within a few months decided to marry. Rita explained that she planned to have a career. Gustave agreed with her plan. In a short time, Gustave left the practice of law and went into business, becoming one of the founders of the cable television industry. Despite her success in law school, Rita had a difficult time finding a job after she graduated in 1959. After many interviews that concluded with "We are not hiring women" or "You could work in wills and estates," she was accepted in the Honors Program at the Justice Department. While in Washington she also worked as a speechwriter and a campaign strategist for Richard Nixon.

The Hausers returned to New York and adopted two children. Rita was hired at Stroock, Stroock, and Lavan. At the time there were no other women in the firm. Using her contacts in Europe from the time she spent in Paris, Rita brought in clients from France. When Nixon was elected in 1969, he asked her to return to Washington as his speechwriter. She decided that a move to Washington with two young children was not advisable and asked him to appoint her to do something at the UN. Rita took some time off from her law firm and served as the American representative to the Human Rights Commission, a post pioneered by Eleanor Roosevelt. In later years she chaired the International Peace Institute at the UN. She was also involved in the effort to rescue Jews from the Soviet Union. She continued to bring international clients to her law firm—Iranians who fled after the shah was deposed, Jordanians, Lebanese, and Israelis.

During her time at the UN, she got to know the Swedish foreign minister who was trying to mediate the Arab-Israeli conflict. He concluded that the Israelis would have to recognize the Palestine Liberation Organization (PLO), at the time deemed a terrorist organization, and that the PLO would have to recognize Israel. Since educational meetings were permitted between the two groups, he asked Hauser to host them in her law office. When asked if she would lead a small delegation of influential American Jews to meet representatives of the PLO in Sweden, Hauser agreed. At this meeting and several subsequent meetings, Hauser met PLO chairman Yasser Arafat. Finally, a declaration was issued in which Arafat denounced terrorism and recognized Israel. The US then recognized the PLO and Israel did too. The meetings moved to Oslo. She also met and befriended Professor Edward Said of Columbia, a supporter of the PLO, after debating with him at the Council on Foreign Relations. Hauser took the position that a two-state solution was the only possible way to peace. Said believed that it would never happen. After his death in 2003, Hauser joined others to fund a chair in Arabic and Comparative Literature in his name at Columbia.

Having remained a lifelong Republican, Hauser broke with her party following America's entry into Iraq. She had served on President George W. Bush's intelligence board and tried to convince him not to invade Iraq. When Barack Obama ran for office, she supported the Republicans for Obama campaign, since he called for getting American forces out of Iraq.

Rita and Gustave Hauser have made significant contributions to NYU and Harvard. At NYU they endowed the Hauser Global Law School and at Harvard they endowed the Leaders in Residence at the Kennedy School. Rita has also made a significant contribution to Hunter's Human Rights program at Roosevelt House. In reminiscing about her time as a Hunter student, Rita explained her attachment to the college:

> In the lunchroom we had a group of us who used to argue about whatever was going on in the world at the time. There was a lot of excitement, a lot of politics. It was an awful time. It was the height of the Cold War and there was real fear that we were going to have a nuclear confrontation. It was a great place. It was a warm place. I have the fondest memories of Hunter, far more than I do of Harvard Law School. Harvard

> Law School was a time of conflict, fighting for every inch of whatever you got and a lot of hostility to women.

In 1956, two years after Rita graduated, Martina Arroyo received her BA from Hunter College at the age of nineteen. Martina was the younger of two children born to Demetrio Arroyo, originally from Puerto Rico, and Lucille Washington, from Charleston, South Carolina. Martina was born in 1937 and grew up in Harlem near Saint Nicholas Avenue and 111th Street. Her father was a mechanical engineer who worked for the Brooklyn Navy Yard. His income allowed the family to experience the cultural riches of New York City. Martina attended concerts and theatrical performances, and frequented museums with her family. While attending Broadway performances in the 1940s she became interested in having a career on the stage. She began to study ballet and piano. She also sang in her church choir and participated in musical events at Hunter College High School where she was a student from 1949 to 1953.

It was while she was in high school that she discovered opera. The Hunter Opera Workshop practiced nearby. One day she got up the courage to ask Joseph Turnau, the director, for an audition. He agreed to listen to her sing. Martina chose the jewel song, "Ah, je ris de me voir si belle," from Charles Gounod's *Faust*. Turnau was impressed by her voice but horrified by her French pronunciation of the song. Martina had learned the French phonetically from a recording. Turnau arranged for her to begin taking lessons at the Opera Workshop while she was in high school. These lessons included basic singing and acting techniques, body movement and dancing, fencing, makeup for stage, costuming, scenic and lighting design, as well as role preparation and diction. He introduced her to Madame Marinka Gurewich, who became her only voice teacher, and to Thea Dispeaker, who became her agent.

Martina continued her studies at Hunter College, majoring in Romance languages, and graduating in 1956. While continuing to study for an operatic career, Martina taught for a year at Draper High School in the Bronx and later was a case worker for the New York City Welfare Department. On January 31, 1958, Martina sang the national anthem at the Waldorf Astoria at an Americans for Democratic Action dinner in honor of FDR's birthday. Adlai Stevenson was the principal speaker. She also sang at the Alumnae Association's birthday luncheon the following month. The alumnae celebrated Martina's performance in their newsletter: "The highly gifted singer, who we hope will join our Regina Resnik in the roster of Metropolitan stars, was Martina Arroyo, Hunter graduate and member of the Hunter College Opera Workshop." On March 30, Martina participated in the Nineteenth Metropolitan Opera Auditions of the Air. She selected "O Patria Mia" from Giuseppe Verdi's *Aida* and was chosen as one of four singers who won the competition. Each winner received $1,000 and a scholarship to study at the Kathryn Long School of the Metropolitan Opera.

At the school, Martina studied singing, drama, German, English diction, and fencing. Her first professional performance, as the First Coryphée in the American premiere of Ildebrando Pizzetti's *Murder in the Cathedral*, was supposed to be performed at a festival upstate. Heavy rain changed the venue to Carnegie Hall. *The New York Times* reported: "Martina Arroyo is a gifted soprano who appears to have remarkable potential, and she sang with a voice of amplitude and lovely color." Six months later Arroyo sang the title role in Christoph Gluck's *Iphigénie en Tauride* in a concert version with the Little Orchestra Society at Town Hall. And two months later she made her Metropolitan Opera debut as the Celestial Voice in Verdi's *Don Carlo*.

She spent several years traveling back and forth to Europe to appear in many small roles in minor opera houses. These roles were interspersed with roles at the Met, singing small roles in Richard Wagner's *Ring Cycle* and Verdi's *Don Carlo*. In 1963, Arroyo was offered a contract to join the Zurich Opera as a principal soprano. She made her debut there in the title role of Verdi's *Aida*. In February 1965, she sang Aida in her first starring role at the Met as a last-minute replacement for Birgit Nilsson. Her performance was met with a standing ovation and with rave reviews in *The New York Times*, which praised Arroyo as "one of the most gorgeous voices before the public today." The Met became her principal home from that point until 1978. She performed music by Giuseppe Verdi, Giacomo Puccini, Wolfgang Amadeus Mozart, Umberto Giordano, Amilcare Ponchielli, and Pietro Mascagni. She was the first Black woman to perform Elsa in Wagner's *Lohengrin*.

During her years at the Met, Arroyo traveled internationally and nationally to perform at other great opera houses. In 1968 she sang in Giacomo Meyerbeer's *Les Huguenots* in Tel Aviv and in London. She later sang in Philadelphia, Chicago, and San Francisco. In 1972, she sang her debut at La Scala, the following year at the Opéra National de Paris and the Teatro Colón in Buenos Aires. By 1980, she became more selective in the roles she agreed to perform. Arroyo demonstrated continuing affection for her alma mater by starring in a gala benefit performance at the Hunter College Playhouse (today the Sylvia and Danny Kaye Playhouse) in 1984. On the stage that had once featured Arthur Rubinstein and Marian Anderson, Martina performed with the Hunter College Symphony Orchestra. She made her last scheduled performance at the Met on October 31, 1986, her 199th performance in the house. In 1991, she came out of retirement for one additional performance in the world premiere of H. Leslie Adams's *Blake*, an opera set in pre–Civil War America.

In 1976, Arroyo was appointed to the National Council of the Arts by President Gerald Ford and served for six years. She also served on the boards of Carnegie Hall, the Metropolitan Opera Guild, Collegiate Choral, and the Hunter College Foundation. She was inducted as a fellow into the American Academy of Arts and Sciences in 2002. She established the Martina Arroyo Foundation in 2003, offering artists at the beginning of their professional careers a curriculum focusing on the preparation of complete operatic roles. In 2010, Martina Arroyo was a recipient of the Opera Honors Award from the National Endowment of the Arts. In 2013, Martina Arroyo was the recipient of Kennedy Center Honors. She was honored for her extraordinary achievements as an artist as well as for sharing her artistry with a new generation of opera singers.

In 1957, one year after Martina Arroyo graduated, *Mademoiselle* featured a profile of Hunter College as part of a series on outstanding colleges and universities. The author, Virginia Voss, pointed out that Hunter students did not have to wait for a vacation trip to take advantage of New York's art museums, libraries, and operas. They had the city for their campus. Voss continued, "Immediately surrounded by the Soviet Mission, by the New York Foundling Home, and by the city's most exclusive men's club, the Union Club, Hunter reflects worldliness from its classroom windows."

In November 1957 Dean Mina Rees published a report on "The State of the College." She noted that the incoming class of freshmen had sixteen hundred students, the largest class in many years. She wrote about the full-time student body of fifty-five hundred with a total of nearly fifteen thousand when part-time, nonmatriculated, and graduate students were included, operating on the two campuses in Manhattan and the Bronx. Graduates had won an impressive number of awards including the New York State Fulbright award to study theatre arts at the Vienna Academy of Music; Fulbright and student exchange fellowships in Italy, France, and Germany; fellowships and teaching fellowships at Cornell, Yale, Chicago, Smith, the University of Michigan, Iowa State, and Temple University

Medical School, and a special award of $2,000 and a year's leave, with pay, to study psychology at Fordham to a graduate who is a member of the New York City Police force. In total, for academic year 1956–1957, 163 awards from 60 institutions were given to 133 students and 6 faculty.

Students who graduated in 1957 left their alma mater with equal measures of confidence and confusion. Their thoughts were captured in the epilogue to their *Wistarion*:

> We're bringing something with us as we step out from the cloister into the maelstrom of the modern world.
>
> We bring independence of thought—thought based on reason and understanding, on perception and cultivated intuition.
>
> We bring our personal philosophies, often saturated with pessimism and despair, but colored with the indispensable radiance of individual hope and aspiration.
>
> We bring religion—dogmatic and liberal—religion that is more than emotion, more than esoteric mist.
>
> We bring science to confusion; and although we may be submerged with the complexities of confusion, the art of science will eventually triumph and bring order, even if it only be to our own personalities.
>
> We bring love—the diffuse love of brothers who have lived to learn and learned to live with each other, pray with each other, communicate with each other. . . .
>
> We bring ambition—sometimes uncertain, sometimes misdirected, sometimes callous; but ambition often leads to greater fulfillment.
>
> We bring service and responsibility to the community of the world—whatever our own limited world may comprise.

They ended with the realization that though they were still young, they were no longer untroubled, no longer innocent, and no longer submissive. They were aware of the space race set off by the launch of the first Russian Earth satellite, *Sputnik I*, in October 1957, followed in January 1958 by the US satellite, *Explorer I*. The 1955 Salk polio vaccine, the 1956 revolution in Hungary, and the 1957 death of Senator Joseph McCarthy were all the subjects of talks given at the college. Among the speakers were President Shuster, Eleanor Roosevelt, and Mayor Robert Wagner.

Hunter students stood nightly with political refugees outside the Russian Embassy and marched in support of Hungarian freedom. In recognition of student interest, Hunter College added a Russian language department.

In 1959 the English Club hosted a reading by the iconoclastic poet Allen Ginsberg. The Cold War grew icier over the division of Berlin by a wall. France devalued the franc to gain economic stability. Fidel Castro and his rebels overthrew the Fulgencio Batista dictatorship in Cuba. Little Rock, Arkansas, was a symbol of national shame as local officials defied federal desegregation orders. Alaska and Hawaii became states. That year, Audre Lorde graduated with a BA in literature and philosophy, following a long leave of absence from college studies.

Audrey (Audre) Geraldine Lorde was born in Harlem in 1934, the third of three daughters, to Caribbean immigrant parents. Her father, Frederick Byron Lorde, was born in Barbados, and her mother, Linda Belmar Lorde, was Grenadian, born on the island of Carriacou. The family struggled to survive during the difficult Depression years. They had little sympathy for the difficulties of their youngest daughter who was born very near-sighted and didn't speak until she was four. Strict rules and physical punishment for disobedience characterized Lorde family life. Despite her problems, Audrey began to demonstrate a precocious ability to memorize poetry. She followed her sisters to Catholic parochial schools through the eighth grade.

In 1947 she entered Hunter College High School where she began writing poetry and connecting with others who thought of themselves as outcasts. There she met Gennie, her first serious friend. Together they played hooky, smoked cigarettes, and forged notes for each other to excuse their absences. They stole nickels from their mothers and roamed Fifth Avenue singing "Solidarity forever, the union makes us strong." They developed a political consciousness, responding to the Berlin airlift, to Mahatma Gandhi's efforts to free India from British control, and to the establishment of the State of Israel, which, they believed, represented a new hope for human dignity. The idyllic times ended abruptly with Gennie's suicide, leaving Audrey, who changed her name to Audre, inconsolable for months.

By the time Audre graduated from high school she had been elected literary editor of the school's art magazine, had published a poem, "Spring," in *Seventeen* magazine, and had participated in poetry workshops sponsored by the Harlem Writers Guild. She remembered her high school years as the first time she met young women, Black and white, who spoke a language she could understand, with whom she shared ideas and feelings without fear. She had teachers who tolerated her ideas and feelings, and some who admired them. These positive experiences were different from the continuing struggle she had at home where her mother's coldness and rigid rules remained in force. At seventeen, just after graduation, Audre moved out to live on her own.

The following year presented a host of difficulties. She earned money to finance her new living arrangements, attended Hunter College, and had an affair with a white man that left her pregnant and in search of an abortion the night before her eighteenth birthday. In search of different solutions, Audre took a leave of absence from Hunter and moved to Stamford, Connecticut, where she found employment in factories and continued her critical observation of her world. The execution of Julius and Ethel Rosenberg in 1953 was shocking to Audre; she recognized the hatred against people who were different or who defied convention, whether as a communist or as a homosexual. Despite her fears, she began her first lesbian relationship with a fellow worker. She saved money diligently with the goal of traveling to Mexico, a place where she hoped to find community.

During the year she spent in Mexico, Audre met and fell in love with Eudora, an American journalist who was twenty years her senior. Audre took classes at the University of Mexico and wrote poetry. Recognizing that Eudora suffered from alcoholism, she left the relationship and returned to New York alone on July 4, 1954. Struggling to find community in Greenwich Village where she was recognized as a Black lesbian, a minority within a minority, she worked as an assistant in a public library. The following summer, she decided to return to Hunter College to finish her degree.

Studying literature and philosophy, Audre submitted pieces to the *Echo*, which published some of her poems and stories, and appointed her to the editorial staff. In "Nothing New Under the Sun," she wrote about herself at the age of twenty-one:

> I've been to Mexico and read Allen Ginsberg and spent Sunday afternoons in Washington Square Park, watching the non-bohemian villagers and the non-Italian bohemians vie for the benches in the shade. I've done Saturday nights on a one-seated table by a coffee-shop window, watching the uptown slummers tripping by, and the village broads with their narrow hips rolling like drunken shovels down the street. I've chased

> and been chased, dug and been dug, till my dwarf-roots are shrieking up out of the pavement on every corner I pass. . . .
> This year, I survive as a teller of tales. . . .

The offices of the *Echo* were adjacent to those of the Student Council. Many students worked late in both offices. In a chance encounter Audre met Blanche Wiesen (Cook), who was active in student government. Their friendship was important to both women who began to socialize with each other at gay bars. What began as a clandestine friendship, lesbian and interracial, as Blanche was white, remained an important relationship, sometimes intimate, until Audre's death.

Lorde graduated from Hunter College in 1959 and began a graduate program in library science at Columbia University. Two years later she received her master of library science degree and found a job as the young adult librarian at the Mount Vernon Library. She also met Edwin Ashley Rollins, a Columbia Law School graduate, at political gatherings, some of which were hosted by old friends from Hunter College High School, on the Upper West Side. Lorde was twenty-seven; Rollins was thirty. Both had had homosexual relationships but wanted to try to build an interracial family; Rollins was white. They married on March 31, 1962, with the intention of having children. The wedding took place at St. Mary's Church on 126th Street. Audre's mother and sisters attended; Ed's family did not attend. A reception was held at Roosevelt House.

Eight of Audre's poems dating from 1952 to 1962 were published in an anthology titled *Sixes and Sevens*. Her introduction to that volume demonstrates growing clarity about her place in the world: "I am a Negro woman and a poet—all three stand outside the realm of choice." A few months after the publication of those poems, in March 1963 Audre gave birth to Elizabeth Marion Lorde-Rollins at New York Hospital in Manhattan, and five months later, on August 28, she and Ed joined the March on Washington. The possibility that racism in America could be ended in her lifetime seemed real to her that day. Four months later, she gave birth to Jonathan Frederick Ashley Rollins. Two more of her poems were published by the end of 1964 in an anthology edited by Langston Hughes, *New Negro Poets*. In 1966, the Lorde-Rollins family moved to 626 Riverside Drive, a three-bedroom apartment overlooking the Hudson River.

In January 1968, Audre received an invitation from the National Endowment for the Arts to become poet-in-residence at Tougaloo College, a historically Black college, in Jackson, Mississippi. Ed offered to take care of the children, and Audre headed south. She was productive in the environment of students who responded to her workshops with admiration and devotion. At Tougaloo, she met Frances Clayton, a white woman psychologist from Brown University. They were deeply attracted to each other and would remain loving partners for decades. In September, reeling from the assassinations of Martin Luther King Jr. and Robert F. Kennedy, Audre accepted a teaching position at City College of New York, in the new SEEK (Search for Education, Elevation and Knowledge) program created to improve the academic skills of the mostly Black students admitted without passing entrance exams. Lorde supported student protests in the following months until she learned of the violence against women that seemed to be part of the movement.

Lorde taught at Lehman College in fall 1969, and she also began marriage counseling sessions with Rollins. A trial separation led to divorce in 1970. Lorde left Lehman and began to teach in the English Department at John Jay College of Criminal Justice, the first Black member of its faculty. She taught a class, Race and the Urban Situation, whose students were Black, Puerto Rican, and uniformed members of the New York Police Department. She became active in discussions about creating a Black studies department. She invited Frances Clayton to live with her. She met and befriended Adrienne Rich and began to think more deeply about feminist issues. In 1973, she came out publicly as a lesbian in a woman-owned bookstore and coffeehouse on West Seventy-Second Street. The poem she read, "Love Poem," was published a few months later in *Ms.* magazine. She posted her poem in the English Department where she was under attack by Black students for her lesbianism. In 1974, a collection of Lorde's poetry, *From a Land Where Other People Live*, was shortlisted for the National Book Award for Poetry, an honor shared by Adrienne Rich, Allen Ginsberg, and Alice Walker.

In 1974, Lorde, Clayton, and Lorde's two children flew to Africa for a five-week tour that included Togo, Ghana, and Dahomey (later the People's Republic of Benin). In public readings that followed her return to the US, she often appeared in a dashiki shirt and a gele, the head wrap of African women, adorned with beads and jewelry. Two years later, she traveled to Russia after being invited by the African Asian Writers' Conference. Four months later, she was in Nigeria as a member of the first American contingent to the Second World Black and African Festival of Arts and Culture (FESTAC '77). Once she returned home, Lorde took on responsibilities as the poetry editor for a new feminist quarterly, *Chrysalis.*

She read thousands of submissions and published many emerging poets. In 1982, she coedited, with Patricia Bell-Scott, *All the Women Are White, All the Blacks Are Men, But Some of Us Are Brave*, a work supporting Black women's studies. She now believed that racism within the women's movement perpetuated the invisibility of Black women as did sexism within the civil rights movement. She used her growing stature to urge Black women to speak up, to transform their silence into language and action.

In September 1978, Lorde learned she had breast cancer. She had a mastectomy and began to write about her experience. A year later, she was the keynote speaker at the first National March on Washington for Lesbian and Gay Rights. The title of her talk was "When Will the Ignorance End?" She addressed the isolation and lack of support she experienced as a Black lesbian. Her *Cancer Journals* were published in September 1980. The following year she joined with a group of women to establish Kitchen Table: Women of Color Press.

In February 1981, Lorde received a letter from the chairman of the English Department at Hunter College inviting her to teach poetry workshop courses in the department's creative writing program. For the next five years, Lorde taught a course on "American Fiction and Poetry Since World War II." It was a study of the writer as outsider in postwar America. While teaching at Hunter she finished and published *Zami: A New Spelling of My Name*. The title was taken from French patois of "les amies" or women friends, pronounced "lay-zami." It was a testament to loving friendships, to African ways of rearing children, to her identification as a Caribbean woman. The celebration for the publication was held at Roosevelt House.

In February 1984, Lorde's cancer spread to her liver. She suffered weakness and pain, but also thought of her legacy. In December 1985, the Audre Lorde Women's Poetry Center was dedicated at Roosevelt House. Lorde died on November 17, 1992, at age fifty-eight in Saint-Croix, Virgin Islands, where she lived her last years with women friends. In 2022, Sixty-Eighth Street between Park and Lexington Avenues, a cross street on the expanded Hunter Campus, was named Audre Lorde Way. Her life was a testament to the Hunter ethic of excellence and activism.

Two years after Audre's graduation, Doris Derby graduated, a member of the class of 1961. Her commitment to activism and the excellence of her professional work are examples of the culture of Hunter College, even as it faced imminent changes. Derby was born in 1939 in Williamsbridge, a neighborhood in the North Bronx that was almost rural at the time. Her parents raised chickens and ducks, grew vegetables, and cultivated fruit trees. Doris's father was a civil servant who had been unable to find a job as a civil engineer, despite his college degree, because of racial prejudice. He later founded an organization to promote the careers of Black civil servants. Her mother worked as a teacher's aide. Doris's great aunt was a missionary in Liberia in the 1940s and 1950s. She sent letters and photographs to Doris's grandparents who read them aloud to Doris, making her aware of African culture.

In elementary school, she visited nearby Michaux's Bookstore, which featured books about Africa and the Caribbean, and she began to write reports about Africa. In junior high school, Doris learned that there was an African dance class in Harlem and that auditions were being held for scholarships to attend the class. Doris won a scholarship and started to study African dance on 135th Street. She continued to write about

Figure 5.3. Doris Derby, 1961. *Source*: Archives and Special Collections, Hunter College Libraries, Hunter College of the City University of New York, New York City.

Africa in high school, visiting the Schomburg Collection and Liberation Bookstore to find more information about Africa. Simultaneously she started to paint on Masonite boards that she found among her father's woodworking supplies.

Doris continued to dance and paint while attending classes at Hunter College where she majored in cultural anthropology and minored in elementary education. She became active in the Anthropology Club, serving as its vice president. During the summer following her sophomore year, Doris was hired to work in a Navajo mission school and hospital in New Mexico. During her junior year she learned from a friend that he was going to Nigeria with the Experiment in International Living. Doris applied and won a scholarship to spend the summer of 1960 in Nigeria. When she returned to Hunter, Doris became part of a group of students who supported the civil rights movement. She joined the group organized by the Student Council that was going to North Carolina, visiting Raleigh, Durham, and Greensboro, talking to people to learn about the sit-in movement started by Black college students to desegregate businesses.

Doris graduated in December 1961 and was immediately hired to teach third grade. She learned that a Hunter classmate, Peggy Dammond, had gone to Albany, Georgia, in the summer of 1962 and that she was in jail and ill. She went south to see if she could help her friend. She moved to Atlanta where she contacted the Student Nonviolent Coordinating Committee (SNCC) office and arranged to be assigned to Albany to help with voter registration. By the time she got there, Peggy had been moved to a jail in Americus, Georgia. Doris returned to New York in the fall to continue teaching and to take some graduate classes at night. She continued to work with SNCC, helping to organize the March on Washington.

In the fall of 1963, Doris was encouraged by SNCC leaders to move to Jackson, Mississippi. Derby developed an adult literacy program; she cofounded the Free Southern Theater; researched the educational outcomes of Black and white students; developed Head Start programs; and led the development of cooperatives to make leather goods, Black rag dolls, baskets, and other local products. She became a marketer for Liberty House, the retail outlet for those wares. In 1968, she joined a Jackson-based initiative called Southern Media, whose mission was to document Black life and to train local Black residents in documentary filmmaking and photography.

At Southern Media Derby began to take photographs of toddlers being examined at health care clinics, and of the doctors and nurses who were caring for them. She filmed older women sewing at quilting cooperatives; she took photos of voters of all ages casting their ballots at local polling places. She took pictures of an adult education math class and of Black elected officials and Black-owned businesses. She photographed people attending political rallies in Black churches. She was one of the few women photographers of the civil rights movement. Photos of the movement were captured mostly by white men working for mainstream media companies. Derby trained her camera on women and children, which gave her work a different character. Her work was included in a 2008 show, *Road to Freedom: Photographs of the Civil Rights Movement, 1956–1968*, at the High Museum of Art in Atlanta.

Derby left Mississippi after nine years and enrolled in a graduate program in anthropology at the University of Illinois at Urbana-Champaign, receiving her MA in 1975 and her PhD in 1980. She joined the faculty teaching anthropology and African American studies there and later taught at the University of Wisconsin in Madison. She later returned to the South, teaching at the College of Charleston in South Carolina. From 1990 until her retirement in 2012 she was the director of the Office of African American Student Services and Programs at Georgia State University. While in Atlanta she joined Sistagraphy, a Black women's photography collective.

In 2021, Derby published *A Civil Rights Journey*, reflecting on her life of activism. She concluded that real progress had not yet been made in Mississippi, despite the energy of the civil rights movement. She observed, "There were few clear-cut gains, just as gains were uneven all over the South." She also pledged to continue the fight: "We are seeing repeats of what we saw back then, like voter suppression and police brutality. When you make strides, the enemy takes steps to block your achievements, and you must do something else." During her long journey, she married Robert A. Banks, an actor, in 1995. Doris Derby died in April 2022 at the age of eighty-two.

During the 1950s, when Senator Joseph McCarthy injected a note of fear in American colleges, President Shuster remained a champion of freedom. Hunter women who graduated in this decade selected from a growing number of majors and dedicated themselves to a wide variety of professional careers. Some, like Florence Howe and Audre Lorde, challenged the academic canon and added new subjects of inquiry. Others, like Mildred Dresselhaus, broke into previously all-male domains of study, while Evelyn Handler became the first woman president of a land-grant college. Still others, like Antonia Pantoja, created new educational institutions to serve previously neglected students. Martina Arroyo became internationally known while Rita Hauser quietly sought to solve international problems and Doris Derby made unique records of the civil rights movement with her camera.

The Legacy of Hunter College

The first men to enroll at Hunter College were veterans of World War II who were admitted to a special program at the Bronx campus in September 1946. The success of the program led to community support for a four-year coeducational division of Hunter College in the Bronx. In 1951, the Bronx campus of Hunter College became coeducational, while Hunter College on Park Avenue remained a women's college. In 1968, after a period of sustained growth, the Bronx campus followed the path of the Brooklyn and Queens annexes, to become an independent college. It was renamed the Herbert H. Lehman College. Each of Hunter's former annexes had become coeducational institutions. City College, founded as a men's school, began to admit women to graduate and business programs in 1930 and became completely coeducational in 1951. Hunter College remained the only public women's college in New York City.

The move to coeducation at the Park Avenue campus of Hunter happened gradually as male students attending the Bronx campus participated in Park Avenue classes that were not available in the Bronx, as well as in many student clubs. The *Bulletin* was renamed the *Arrow* in 1949 at the urging of veterans who had joined the editorial staff. In recognition of the men who graduated from the Bronx campus of Hunter, the Alumnae Association of Hunter College officially changed its name to the Alumni Association in 1955.

Hunter's reputation as a women's college remained strong throughout the 1950s. Klara Apat (Silverstein), a student at Erasmus Hall High School, remembered thinking about applying to Hunter College. Though most of her friends planned to attend Brooklyn College, which was closer to their homes, Klara thought of the opportunity for leadership she would have at Hunter. Nine years before Betty Friedan published *The Feminine Mystique*, beginning the women's movement, Klara knew that she wanted to be a leader. She knew that she could become the president of a student club at a women's college, while at a coeducational college, at best, she could become a club secretary. Klara enrolled at Hunter and realized the opportunity she sought, becoming president of Hunter's Hillel Club. She credits its director, Toby Lelyveld, for being a major mentor. As president, Klara was invited to participate in a Harvard-Princeton-Yale Hillel colloquium where her leadership skills were honed in small discussion sessions and votes on policy decisions. Following graduation in 1954, Klara Apat Silverstein used those leadership skills in elementary school teaching as well as in a long career of volunteer philanthropy.

In 1961, Student Council president Blanche Wiesen (Cook) invited Eleanor Roosevelt, long affiliated with Hunter College, to speak. Roosevelt delivered a rousing message about civil rights. Blanche recalled her comments: "Many changes are going on in this country now and there is a fabulous student movement. People are demanding justice and integration and an end to the cruelty and bitterness of segregation." Roosevelt encouraged Hunter students to go to the South for freedom, to see for themselves. Within weeks the Student Council had hired two buses to take students to North Carolina. Blanche reported that they witnessed unimaginable horrors—segregation in all aspects of public life. She noted that Roosevelt had a great capacity for empathy and that Hunter students learned from her to be active, to never give up, to learn everything they could, and to question authority. During her two decades of involvement with Hunter students Eleanor Roosevelt's message was consistent, recalled Cook: "Don't believe the headlines, do your own research, get out there, be an activist, participate in the world around you. . . . Live fully and live free." Florence Rosenfeld Howe and Doris Derby as well as legions of others did just that. Blanche Wiesen Cook became a historian and wrote a three-volume biography of Eleanor Roosevelt.

Tens of thousands of women graduated from Hunter during its century of existence as a women's college. Hunter alumnae have brought honor to the college in many fields of endeavor. In its early decades, thousands became teachers in the public schools of New York City. Hunter is the only college to have graduated two women Nobel laureates, both in medicine, Gertrude Elion, who majored in chemistry, and Rosalyn Sussman Yalow, who majored in physics. Hunter's emphasis on civic activism led two graduates, Edna Flannery Kelly and Bella Savitsky Abzug, to serve as congresswomen. Hunter students also benefited from opportunities to participate in college journalism. Writing skills and determination opened careers for S. F. Porter in financial journalism, Rose Franzblau in family advice columns, Ada Louise Huxtable in architectural journalism, and Judith Crist in film criticism. All Hunter students benefited from the cultural riches of New York City. Two of them, Regina Resnik and Martina Arroyo, became stars at the Metropolitan Opera.

The City University of New York, CUNY, a consortium of public colleges, was established by state legislation in 1961. It included City, Hunter, Brooklyn, Queens, and the Graduate Center. (Lehman College was added in 1968.) The Board of Higher Education, renamed the CUNY Board of Trustees, was its governing body. A few years after the creation of CUNY, Hunter College continued its gradual transition to coeducation. In 1964 it admitted 426 male freshmen, a minor presence among the 8,360 students registered in the day session that year. The *Wistarion* of 1964 included a comic graphic image of a poster advocating "Ban the Boys." Women remained in leadership roles in the administration, faculty, and the student body. Admission at Hunter in the sixties was limited to students who achieved a 92 GPA in high school. The dual goal of excellence and activism continued to be reflected in student publications and in club programs.

In 1967, Mary Gambrell, professor of history, dean of the faculty, and Hunter's first woman president, restated the educational philosophy of the college in the student newspaper, the *Envoy,* which had replaced the *Arrow*: "Their (student) education is designed to develop personal potential to meet whatever situation new worlds may present. They are not misled into preparing to fit a slot that beckons today. They know well that tomorrow will be different and will be superseded by yet another tomorrow." Hunter students had participated in the major issues of their times—the free kindergarten movement, settlement houses, and support for soldiers in World War I in the teens and 1920s, peace strikes in the 1930s, the war effort of the 1940s, and opposition to McCarthyism in the 1950s.

In the 1960s, Hunter student activists joined students from all CUNY schools to oppose racial discrimination. They questioned and ultimately rejected the policy of admitting only those with high grade point averages in high school, since the policy created a student body that did not reflect the demography of New York City. An "Open Admissions" policy was demanded by CUNY students to enable more Black and Hispanic students to benefit from free college education. The policy was adopted by the CUNY Board of Trustees and put into practice in 1970. Achieving academic excellence remained a goal, necessitating new programs to support students who were admitted without college-ready skills. As these programs were developing, the 1975 fiscal crisis in New York led to the abrupt end of free tuition at CUNY. In response to tuition charges, the Alumni Scholarship and Welfare Fund moved swiftly to increase financial help to Hunter undergraduates.

Coeducation, open admissions, and tuition charges posed fundamental challenges to the established character of Hunter College. Nevertheless, curricular programs that were initiated at the college in the 1960s provide evidence that student interest continued to reflect the culture established by earlier generations of students and faculty. A Teacher Education Program was established to give students a fifth year of training, leading to a master of arts in education. An Urban Research Center, reflecting early student involvement in social services, was created in 1962. The first master of fine arts degree was offered by Hunter's distinguished Art Department. The Thomas Hunter Scholars Program was established in 1964, building on the honors classes enjoyed by Florence Howe and Rita Hauser in the 1950s. In 1967, the Bellevue School of Nursing was transferred to Hunter College, and the Institute of Health Sciences was founded in 1969.

The legacy of the first century of Hunter College is visible in its continued presence on several sites in Manhattan, including the three main campuses as well as several additional facilities. The original campus sprawls from Sixty-Eighth to Sixty-Ninth Streets, between Park and Lexington Avenues, and has spilled across Lexington into two towers; bridges connect the East and West buildings, and a bridge connects the West building to the North building. Adjacent to this campus are the Baker Theatre on East Sixty-Seventh Street; Casa Lally, Hunter's Italian institute, on East Sixty-Fifth Street; and Roosevelt House, housing the public policy institute, further west on East Sixty-Fifth Street. The Belfer Research Building located on East Sixty-Ninth Street houses biomedical research in cooperation with the Weill Cornell Medical College. The second main campus houses the Hunter Campus Schools, including both the elementary school and the high school. It is located between Park and Madison Avenues, and between East Ninety-Fourth and East Ninety-Fifth Streets. Continuing uptown, the East Harlem Campus, Hunter's newest campus, is at 119th Street and Third Avenue, housing the Silberman School of Social Work, CENTRO (Center for Puerto Rican Studies), and Nutrition and Public Health. Downtown, the Brookdale Campus on Twenty-Fifth

Street and First Avenue, home to the School of Nursing and the School of Health Sciences, is scheduled for major renewal. Further downtown, on Hudson Street, the MFA building has studio and gallery space.

In the fall of 2022, I taught my last class, Writing Women's Biography, for the History Department at Hunter College. The class, an honors seminar, met weekly in the Hunter Archives. At the first meeting, an archivist introduced the students to the system of finding aids established to organize the thousands of boxes of documents that are available for use by researchers. She gave students the opportunity to peruse some boxes of papers deposited by alumnae and to consult volumes of the *Wistarion*. I was delighted with the keen interest expressed by the class in the students of earlier decades. They were fascinated by the photos in the yearbook, intrigued by the school spirit, and impressed by the literary merits of the student writers of prior decades. The major assignment for the semester was to write a brief biography of a Hunter alumna whose papers were in the Hunter Archives or available elsewhere in the city. Students were encouraged to seek opportunities to conduct an oral interview with alumnae or with people who remembered them.

During the semester, each seminar participant shared progress reports with the class. Their first task was to identify an alumna to study. The selection process reflected the wide variety of interests in the group. A senior who wished to study law selected Soia Mentschikoff; another who studied economics selected S. F. Porter. A recent transfer student from a community college selected Antonia Pantoja. A future teacher selected Rita Sommerville Morgan. Several English majors selected writers including Judith Klein Crist, Mim Kolkin Kelber, and Pauli Murray. A history major selected Edna Flannery Kelly. Several students were attracted to the lives of alumnae in the arts including Pearl Primus, Martina Arroyo, and Ruby Dee. The next task was to discuss the materials they found in the archives—letters, publicity materials, reports, and memoirs. Some discovered additional archival holdings, others scheduled oral interviews, and some found published materials.

The students' final papers demonstrate the lasting influence of Hunter College on the remarkable students of earlier decades. The papers are also vivid testimony to the fact that today's students benefit from knowledge of the struggles and successes of their predecessors, students who were imbued with the Hunter culture. Thomas Hunter and the faculty, students, and alumnae of the college established a welcoming community for all the girls of New York City. Changes brought on by new policies in the 1960s and 1970s, coeducation, open admissions, and the end to free tuition, had an influence on Hunter's historical culture but that culture remains central to the character of the college. Today, a preponderance of women in undergraduate classes (about 68 percent in 2024) and in leadership positions in the college are reminders of Hunter's history as the largest women's college in the world. Hunter remains a cosmopolitan campus with twenty-five thousand students from every corner of the world as well as strivers from every borough of the city who are drawn to Manhattan to study. More than 150 years after its founding, Hunter College continues to offer opportunities to New York's diverse population to study a wide variety of fields in preparation for meaningful lives.

References

Archives and Special Collections, Hunter College Libraries

General Collections

A Selected History of the Hunter College Collection, 1914–2017
Alumnae/Alumni Collection, 1872–2017
Concert Bureau Collection, 1943–1976
Hunter College Publications Collection, 1870–2015
Hunter College Student Clubs, Organizations, and Publications, 1871–2016
Lenox Hill Neighborhood House Collection, 1892–2015
Normal College of the City of New York Collection, 1870–1914
Opera Association, 1946–1972
Sara Delano Roosevelt Memorial House Collection, 1943–1992

Individual Collections

Edna Wells Luetz Papers, 1916–1961
Helen Gray Cone Collection, 1859–1934
E. Adelaide Hahn Collection, 1893–1967
LaWanda Cox Papers, 1930–2002
Beatrice Hyslop Papers, 1939–1972
Kate Simon Collection, 1959–1989
Rita Sommerville Morgan, 1946–1990
President George N. Shuster Collection, 1939–1960
President Eugene A. Colligan Collection, 1933–1940
President James M. Kieran Collection, 1929–1933
President George S. Davis Collection, 1908–1938
President Joseph A. Gillet Collection, 1906–1908

Departmental Collections

Art, 1908–2018
Biological Sciences, 1908–1961
Bureau of Educational and Vocational Guidance, 1910–1990
Chemistry, 1933–1962
Classics, 1908–1965
Education, 1908–1956
English, 1908–1971
Health and Physical Education, 1908–1911, 1929–1960
History, 1908–1990
Home Economics, 1943–1967
Music, 1913–1955
Romance Languages, 1911–1971
Sociology and Anthropology, 1942–1979
Speech and Dramatics, 1922–1960

Roosevelt House Oral Interviews

Helene B. Goldfarb
Elaine Small Klein
Regina Resnick
Rita Hauser
Klara Silverstein

Additional archival sources were consulted as follows:

CUNY Graduate School Archives—Mina Rees
Center for Jewish History Archives—Virginia Snitow
NYU Archives—Marion W. Starling
Rose Center Archives, Emory University—Marion W. Starling

Published Sources

Memoirs, Biographies, and Autobiographies

Abzug, Bella S. *Bella! Mrs. Abzug Goes to Washington*, Edited by Mel Ziegler. Saturday Review Press, 1972.
Bell-Scott, Patricia. *The Firebrand and the First Lady: Portrait of a Friendship.* Vintage Books, 2017.

Blantz, Thomas E. *George N. Shuster: On the Side of Truth.* University of Notre Dame Press, 1993.

Davis, Ossie, and Ruby Dee. *With Ossie and Ruby: In This Life Together.* William Morrow, 1998.

Dawidowicz, Lucy. *From That Time and Place: Memoir, 1938–1947.* Introduction by Nancy Sinkoff. Rutgers University Press, 2008.

Derby, Doris. *A Civil Rights Journey.* Mack, 2021.

DeVaux, Alexis. *Warrior Poet: A Biography of Audre Lorde.* W.W. Norton, 2004.

Dodd, Bella V. *School of Darkness.* P.J. Kenedy and Sons, 1954.

Epstein, Dorothy. *A Song of Social Significance: Memoirs of an Activist.* Ben Yehuda Press, 2007.

Howe, Florence. *A Life in Motion.* Feminist Press, 2011.

Kelly, Jason. "Legal Light: Soia Mentschikoff." *Chicago Maroon*, March 27, 2019. https://www.law.uchicago.edu/news/legal-light.

Koppel, Lily. *The Red Leather Diary.* Harper Collins, 2008.

Levine, Suzanne Braun, and Mary Thom. *Bella Abzug.* Farrar, Straus and Giroux, 2007.

Lorde, Audre. *Zami: A New Spelling of My Name.* Persephone Press, 1982.

Matsushita, Marimi. "A Woman Mathematician and Her Contributions: Mina Spiegel Rees." PhD diss., Teachers College, Columbia, 1998.

Murray, Pauli. *Proud Shoes: The Story of an American Family.* Beacon Press, 1999.

Murray, Pauli. *Song in a Weary Throat: Memoir of an American Pilgrimage.* Liveright, 2018.

Oestreich, Alan. "Centennial History of African-Americans in Radiology." *American Journal of Radiology*, 1996.

Pantoja, Antonia. *A Memoir of a Visionary: Antonia Pantoja.* Arte Publico Press, 2002.

Perkins, Linda M. *To Advance the Race: Black Women's Higher Education from the Antebellum Era to the 1960s.* University of Illinois Press, 2024.

Requa, Amos Conklin. *The Family of Requa: 1678–1898.* Peekskill, New York, 1898.

Rosenberg, Rosalind. *Jane Crow: The Life of Pauli Murray.* Oxford University Press, 2017.

Schwartz, Peggy, and Murray Schwartz. *The Dance Claimed Me: A Biography of Pearl Primus.* Yale University Press, 2011.

Shuster, George Nauman. *The Ground I Walked On: Reflections of a College President.* Farrar, Straus, and Cudahy, 1961.

Simon, Kate. *Bronx Primitive: Portraits in a Childhood.* Viking Press, 1982.

Simon, Kate. *Etchings in an Hourglass.* Harper and Row, 1990.

Simon, Kate. *A Wider World: Portraits in an Adolescence.* Harper and Row, 1986.

Sinkoff, Nancy. *From Left to Right: Lucy Dawidowicz, the New York Intellectuals, and the Politics of Jewish History.* Wayne State University Press, 2020.

Weinstock, Maia. *Carbon Queen: The Remarkable Life of Nanoscience Pioneer Mildred Dresselhaus.* MIT Press, 2022.

Women in Congress: 1917–2006. Office of History and Preservation, U.S. House of Representatives, U.S. Government Printing Office, 2006.

History of Hunter College

Burns, Mae A. "An Historical Background and Philosophical Criticism of the Curriculum of Hunter College, 1870–1938." PhD diss., Fordham College, 1938.

The Echo: Journal of the Hunter College Archives in Celebration of the 125th Anniversary of Hunter College. Hunter College, 1995.

Holzer, Harold, ed. *Hunter 150: Celebrating the Past, Caring for the Future.* Hunter College, 2020.

Grunfeld, Katherina Kroo. "Purpose and Ambiguity: The Feminine World of Hunter College, 1869–1945." PhD diss., Teachers College, Columbia, 1991.

Patterson, Samuel White. *Hunter College: Eighty-Five Years of Service.* Lantern Press, 1955.

Williams, Joan M. *Hunter College.* Arcadia Publishing, 2000.

General Background

Alpern, Sara, Joyce Antler, Elisabeth Israels Perry, and Ingrid Winther Scobie, eds. *The Challenge of Feminist Biography: Writing the Lives of American Women.* University of Illinois Press, 1992.

Antler, Joyce. *The Journey Home: Jewish Women and the American Century.* Free Press, 1997.

Eagan, Eileen. *Class, Culture, and the Classroom: The Student Peace Movement of the 1930s.* Temple University Press, 1981.

Eisenmann, Linda. *Higher Education for Women in Postwar America, 1945–1965.* Johns Hopkins University Press, 2006.

Ewen, Elizabeth. *Immigrant Women in the Land of Dollars: Life and Culture on the Lower East Side, 1890–1925.* Monthly Review Press, 1985.

Gordon, Lynn. *Gender and Higher Education in the Progressive Era.* Yale University Press, 1990.

Herman, Debra. "College and After: The Vassar Experiment in Women's Education, 1861–1924." PhD diss., Stanford University, 1979.

Lefkowitz-Horowitz, Helen. *Alma Mater: Design and Experience in Women's Colleges, from Their Nineteenth Century Beginnings to the 1930s.* University of Massachusetts Press, 1993.

Malkiel, Nancy Weiss. *Keep the Damned Women Out: The Struggle for Coeducation.* Princeton University Press, 2016.

Markowitz, Ruth Jacknow. *My Daughter the Teacher: Jewish Teachers in the New York City Schools.* Rutgers University Press, 1993.

Rosenberg, Rosalind. *Changing the Subject: How the Women of Columbia Shaped the Way We Think About Sex and Politics.* Columbia University Press, 2004.

Rosenberg, Rosalind. "The Limits of Access: The History of Coeducation in America." In *Women and Higher Education: Essays from the Mount Holyoke Sesquicentennial Symposia*, edited by John Mack Faragher and Florence Howe. W.W. Norton, 1988.

Rossiter, Margaret W. "Women Scientists in America." *Bulletin of the American Academy of Arts and Sciences* 36, no. 6 (March 1983): 10–16.

Schrecker, Ellen W. *No Ivory Tower: McCarthyism and the Universities.* Oxford University Press, 1986.

Seller, Maxine Schwartz. "A History of Women's Education in the United States: Thomas Woody's Classic, Sixty Years Later." *History of Education Quarterly* 29, no. 1 (Spring 1989): 95–107.

Solomon, Barbara Miller. *In the Company of Educated Women.* Yale University Press, 1985.

Ware, Susan. *Holding Their Own: American Women in the 1930s.* Twayne, 1982.

Ware, Susan. *Letter to the World: Seven Women Who Shaped the American Century.* W.W. Norton, 1998.

Wechsler, James. *Revolt on the Campus.* University of Washington Press, 1973.

Woloch, Nancy. *The Insider: A Life of Virginia C. Gildersleeve.* Columbia University Press, 2022.

Index

Page numbers in *italics* refer to illustrations.

www.ingramcontent.com/pod-product-compliance
Lightning Source LLC
LaVergne TN
LVHW010614100826
845148LV00014B/2959